INTRODUCING THE

JAVA 2 ™

PLATFORM

INTRODUCING THE

JAVA 2

PLATFORM

David Flanagan

O'REILLY®

Beijing • Cambridge • Köln • Paris • Sebastopol • Taipei • Tokyo

Introducing the Java 2 Platform

by David Flanagan

Copyright © 1999 O'Reilly & Associates, Inc. All rights reserved.
Printed in the United States of America.

Published by O'Reilly & Associates, Inc., 101 Morris Street, Sebastopol, CA 95472.

Editor: Paula Ferguson

Production Editor: Nancy Wolfe Kotary

Printing History:

February 1999:   First Edition.

This booklet is printed on acid-free paper with 85% recycled content, 15% post-consumer waste. O'Reilly & Associates is committed to using paper with the highest recycled content available consistent with high quality.

Table of Contents

Preface .... *vii*

1: An Overview of the Java 2 Platform *1*

What Is Java? *1*
Key Benefits of Java *3*
Java 2 or Java 1.2? *5*
Core Features of Java 2 .... *6*
User Interface Features *9*
Graphics Features *19*
Enterprise Features *23*
But Wait, There's More! *27*

2: How to Use the CD-ROM *29*

Contents of the Atlas *29*
Opening the Atlas *30*
Navigating the Atlas *31*
Searching the Atlas *31*
The Platform Map *34*
Package Maps *34*
Class Maps *35*

Index *47*

Preface

This CD-ROM, and the booklet that accompanies it, are a response to the remarkable growth in size and scope of the Java platform.

When Java 1.0 was released, it contained 212 classes and interfaces, grouped into 8 packages. That was a very manageable size. I wrote some tools to extract API information about those classes, wrote up a paragraph or two about each class, and the book *Java in a Nutshell* (O'Reilly & Associates) was born. I added some introductory chapters and some examples to help people who were making the transition to Java, but at its core, the book was meant to be a quick reference. To my surprise and pleasure, the book was wildly successful. Part of its success was its timing and its price. But I believe there was more to it than that.

I've always thought of *Java in a Nutshell* as a quick reference; the book makes no attempt to be a comprehensive source of definitive documentation. As a programmer, what I found appealing about *Java in a Nutshell* was that it was compact yet complete—complete in the sense of covering the entire Java API. For many programmers, *Java in a Nutshell* became the programming resource of first resort. If you needed to look something up, to get the correct name of a method or its exact signature, for example, you'd turn to *Java in a Nutshell* first. Then, if you needed futher details, you'd turn to a more comprehensive reference, such as Sun's online API documentation.

With Java 1.1, the Java platform grew to include 504 classes and interfaces grouped into 23 packages—more than double the size of the initial release. Java was getting too big to fit into a nutshell anymore. After much discussion, my editor and I decided to remove many of the programming examples from *Java in a Nutshell* and make them part of a new book, *Java Examples in a Nutshell* (O'Reilly). But this wasn't enough—Java 1.1 still did not fit into a nutshell. So we made the reluctant decision to omit the new Java 1.1 Enterprise APIs from the second edition of the book. This edition of the book continued to be useful to many programmers, and it continued to be quite successful. But it was no longer complete; it had lost something.

The growth of Java has continued. The Java 2 platform contains 1520 classes and interfaces in 59 packages. This is three times as large as Java 1.1, and seven times as large as the initial release that fit so nicely in a nutshell. And that is before counting the important standard extensions that are now in common use. After adding in the extensions available today, the Java platform grows to 98 packages and well over 2000 classes and interfaces. This is a complete order of magnitude larger than Java 1.0!

To handle this growth, we've had to transform *Java in a Nutshell* into "Java in several nutshells." This process is already underway, with work proceeding on *Java Foundation Classes in a Nutshell* and *Java Enterprise in a Nutshell*. I expect that these will be useful books, and I hope that they will be well received by the many fans of *Java in a Nutshell*. But they won't, and can't, be the same as a single book that covers the entire Java platform.

That is where this CD-ROM and the accompanying booklet come in. I wanted to create a *complete* Java quick-reference solution—a new "resource of first resort" for Java programmers. The Java platform has grown so large that you can easily get lost or bogged down in it. You could spend years programming with it, only to realize that it includes APIs you've never even heard of. I wanted to somehow put Java back into its nutshell, to allow programmers to survey Java from a higher level of abstraction, to let them see that despite its vast size, it still forms a coherent, unified whole. I am a believer in learning by exploring and doing, so I wanted to create a tool that would guide users, yet allow them to explore the Java 2 platform on their own. And that is how the *Java Power Reference* was born.

This booklet is a high-level survey of the entire Java 2 platform, including many of the standard extensions that are in use as this book goes to press. The CD-ROM contains quick-reference material for all of the packages and all of the classes in that platform. The quick-reference material uses the format popularized by *Java in a Nutshell*, but improves upon it and adapts it to the interactive medium of the Web. In particular, the *Java Power Reference* adds searching and hyperlinking capabilities that simply cannot exist in a printed book like *Java in a Nutshell*.

Since the Java platform has grown in size by an order of magnitude, any quick reference that covers the whole platform must do so at a fairly high level or it will simply become too large to be useful. So, while *Java in a Nutshell* contains a paragraph or two about each class and interface, the *Java Power Reference* contains a paragraph or two about each package. For each class and interface, you'll find a complete, well-organized API synopsis, but no textual description. That is still the job for *Java in a Nutshell* and its fothcoming companion volumes.

I want to emphasize that the *Java Power Reference* does not replace *Java in a Nutshell* or the forthcoming companion volumes. It merely usurps the position of *Java in a Nutshell* as the quick reference of first resort.

How the Quick Reference Is Generated

For those nerdy or simply inquisitive readers, this section explains a bit about how the quick-reference material in the *Java Power Reference* was created.

As Java has evolved, so has my system for generating Java quick-reference material. The current system is part of a larger documentation browser system I'm developing. (Visit *http://www.davidflanagan.com/Jude/* for more information about it.) The program works in three passes: the first pass collects and organizes the API information and the second and third passes turn that information into a CD-ROM full of HTML files.

The first pass begins by reading the class files for all of the classes and interfaces to be documented. Almost all of the API information in the quick reference is available in these class files. The notable exception is argument names, which are not stored in class files. These argument names are obtained by parsing the Java source file for each class and interface. Where source files are not available, I obtain method argument names by parsing the API documentation generated by *javadoc*. The parser I use to extract API information from the source files and *javadoc* files is created using the Antlr parser generator developed by Terrence Parr of the Magelang Institute. (See *http://www.antlr.org* for details on this very powerful programming tool.)

Once API information has been obtained by reading class files, source files, and *javadoc* files, the program spends some time sorting and cross-referencing everything. Then it stores all the API information into a single large data file.

The next pass is fairly boring. The program reads API information out of the data file, one class at a time, and prints that API information out in hyperlinked HTML format. The results look impresive enough, but the code that creates those results is tedious!

The third pass is more interesting. The program reads the names of all packages, classes, methods, and fields, sorts them alphabetically, and generates a bunch of JavaScript code. It is this code, stored in many files on the CD-ROM, that makes the CD searchable.

All this processing takes time. The first pass takes the longest, largely because it has to parse all those source files. On my embarassingly slow 150 Mhz Pentium-class system, I've got time for two or three cups of coffee while I wait for the program to process the complete Java platform. And it eats up memory, too. When Java 2 was released, I had to upgrade from 64 MB of RAM to 128 MB in order for the program to run.

Related Books

O'Reilly publishes a lot of books about Java. One way to think about them is in a pyramid-like arrangement. The *Java Power Reference* is at the apex of the pyramid—it covers the complete Java platform at a relatively high level of abstraction.

At the next level are *Java in a Nutshell*, *Java Foundation Classes in a Nutshell*, *Java Enterprise in a Nutshell*, and *Java Examples in a Nutshell*. These books are still quick references, but they contain more detail than the *Java Power Reference*, and each one covers only a subset of the Java platform.

At the base of the pyramid are the many other books in the O'Reilly Java series. These books are tutorials, not quick references. Each book concerns a single topic or API and covers that topic in complete detail. The current and forthcoming titles in this series are the following:

Exploring Java, by Patrick Niemeyer and Joshua Peck
A comprehensive tutorial that provides a practical, hands-on approach to learning Java.

Java Swing, by Robert Eckstein, Marc Loy, and Dave Wood
A complete guide to using all of the user-interface classes in the Swing toolkit.

Java 2D Graphics, by Jonathan Knudsen
A comprehensive tutorial on the Java 2D API, from basic drawing techniques to advanced image processing and font handling.

Java Servlet Programming, by Jason Hunter with William Crawford
A guide to writing servlets that covers dynamic web content, maintaining state information, session tracking, database connectivity using JDBC, and applet-servlet communication.

Java I/O, by Elliotte Rusty Harold
A complete tutorial on all of the input/output facilities available in Java.

Java Security, by Scott Oaks
An advanced guide to all of Java's security features.

Java Cryptography, by Jonathan Knudsen
A complete tutorial on writing secure programs using Java's cryptographic tools.

Java Distributed Computing, by Jim Farley
A programmer's guide to writing distributed applications with Java.

Database Programming with JDBC and Java, by George Reese
An advanced tutorial on JDBC that presents a robust model for developing Java database programs.

Developing Java Beans, by Robert Englander
A complete guide to writing components that work with the JavaBeans API.

Java Native Methods, by Alligator Descartes
An advanced guide to writing native code that works with Java.

Java Threads, by Scott Oaks and Henry Wong
An advanced programming guide to working with threads in Java.

Java Network Programming, by Elliotte Rusty Harold
A complete guide to writing sophisticated network applications.

Java Language Reference, by Mark Grand
A complete reference for the Java programming language itself.

Java AWT Reference, by John Zukowski
A complete reference manual for the AWT-related packages in the core Java API.

Java Fundamental Classes Reference, by Mark Grand and Jonathan Knudsen
   A complete reference manual for the `java.lang`, `java.io`, `java.net`, and `java.util` packages, among others, in the core Java API.

Java Virtual Machine, by Jon Meyer and Troy Downing
   A programming guide and reference manual for the Java Virtual Machine.

Acknowledgments

As always, my editor, Paula Ferguson, has done a bang-up job of keeping me on track, making my prose presentable, and generally handling lots of scutwork. My deep gratitude to her. Lorrie LeJeune and Linda Walsh at O'Reilly played important roles in the birth of this unique CD-ROM quick reference. Their support and encouragement made this project go forward. Edie Freedman worked closely with me to provide the graphics that appear on the CD-ROM. Her design talent is evident in both the printed and electronic portions of this product.

I had a crack team of O'Reilly authors as technical reviewers for the API quick reference. My thanks to Bob Eckstein, Jonathan Knudsen, Allen McPherson, and John Zukowski. While these guys looked over the CD-ROM reference material, Marc Loy reviewed this booklet. My thanks also to him. Bob, Jonathan, and Allen also created the figures that appear in Chapter 1 and were generous enough to allow them to be used for this project.

I'd also like to thank the many readers of *Java in a Nutshell* for making that book so successful. I hope that you find the *Java Power Reference* just as useful to you. In particular, I'd like to thank the hundreds of readers to who took the time to fill out my survey about the API quick-reference format. Based on your feedback, I've substantially improved the *Java in a Nutshell* quick-reference style for this new product.

Finally, I'd like to thank Christie, whose support means so much to me.

   David Flanagan
   http://www.davidflanagan.com
   January 1999

CHAPTER 1

An Overview of the
Java 2 Platform

Welcome to the next generation of Java.

In early December 1998, Sun Microsystems launched the Java 2 platform, a major new release of the Java APIs (application programmer interfaces). Java 2 is a vast improvement upon previous releases: new graphics, user interface, and enterprise capabilities make it three times as large as Java 1.1, and over seven times as large as the initial Java 1.0 release. Despite its rapid growth, Java 2 is well-designed, well-tested, fast, and robust. Java 2 marks the maturity of the Java platform.

This chapter offers a quick overview of the newly mature Java 2 platform.

What Is Java?

When we speak of Java, it is important to distinguish between the Java programming language and the Java platform. The Java programming language is the language in which Java applications, applets, servlets, and components are (usually) written. The Java platform, on the other hand, is the predefined set of Java classes that exist on every Java installation; these classes are available for use by those applications, applets, servlets, and components. The Java platform is also sometimes referred to as the "core Java APIs" or the "Java runtime environment." The Java platform can also be extended with optional standard extensions. These APIs exist in some Java installations, but are not guaranteed to exist in all installations.

The Java Programming Language

The Java programming language is a state-of-the-art, object-oriented language that has a classic syntax similar to that of C. The designers strived to make the Java language powerful, and at the same time tried to avoid the overly complex features that have bogged down other promising object-oriented languages such as C++. By keeping the language simple, the designers also made it easier for programmers to write bug-free and robust code.

1

As a result of its elegant design and next-generation features, the Java language has proved to be wildly popular with programmers, who typically find it a pleasure to work with Java after struggling with more difficult and less powerful languages.

The Java Platform

Just as important as the Java programming language is the Java platform. This is the set of predefined classes that programs written in the Java language rely on. These predefined classes are the building blocks of all Java applications, applets, servlets, and components. Java classes are grouped into related groups known as *packages*. The Java platform defines packages for functions such as input/output, networking, graphics, user interface creation, security, and much more. The bulk of this chapter is devoted to a package-by-package exploration of the full capabilities of the Java 2 platform.

Before we proceed with our survey of the Java platform, however, it is important to understand what is meant by the term "platform." To a computer programmer, a platform is defined by the APIs that he or she can use and rely on when writing programs. These APIs are typically defined primarily by the operating system of the target computer. Thus, a programmer writing a program to run under Microsoft Windows must use a different set of APIs than a programmer writing the same program for the Macintosh or a programmer writing for a Unix-based system. Windows, Macintosh, and Unix are three distinct platforms.

Java is not an operating system.* Nevertheless, the Java platform—particularly the Java 2 platform—provides APIs with a comparable breadth and depth to those defined by an operating system. With the advent of the Java 2 platform, programmers can choose to write applications on the Java platform without sacrificing the advanced features that are available to programmers writing native applications targeted at a particular underlying operating system.

An application written on the Java platform runs on any operating system that supports the Java platform. This means that programmers do not have to create distinct Windows, Macintosh, and Unix versions of their programs. A single Java program runs on all of these operating systems. This explains why "Write once, run anywhere" is Sun's motto for Java.

It also explains why companies such as Microsoft might feel threatened by Java. The Java platform is not an operating system, but for programmers, it is an alternative development target, and a very popular one at that. The Java platform reduces programmers' reliance on the underlying operating system, and by allowing programs to run on top of any operating system, it increases end users' freedom to choose any operating system they prefer.

---

* There is a Java-based operating system, however. It is known as JavaOS.

Key Benefits of Java

Why use Java at all? Why is it worth learning a new language and a new platform? This section explores some of the key benefits of Java.

Write Once, Run Anywhere

Sun identifies "Write once, run anywhere" as the "core value proposition" of the Java platform. Translated from business jargon, this means that the most important promise of Java technology is that you have to write your application only once, for the Java platform, and you'll be able to run it *anywhere*.

Anywhere, that is, that supports the Java platform. Fortunately, Java support is becoming ubiquitous. It is integrated, or being integrated, into practically all major operating systems. It is built into major web browsers, which places it on virtually every Internet-connected PC in the world. It is even being built into consumer electronic devices, such as television set top boxes, PDAs, and cell phones.

Java has been criticized for failing to live up to the promise of "Write once, run anywhere." With the introduction of Swing, the new platform-independent graphical user interface system, however, the Java 2 platform has taken a giant step closer to this goal. And to keep things in perspective, it is important to remember that Java is the only platform that comes anywhere close to meeting the promise of "Write once, run anywhere".

Security

Another key benefit of Java is its security features. The language and the platform were designed from the ground up with security in mind. The Java platform allows users to download untrusted applet code over a network, and to run it in a secure environment in which it cannot do any harm: it cannot infect the host system with a virus, cannot read or write files from the hard drive, and so forth. This capability alone makes the Java platform unique.

The Java 2 platform takes the security model a step further. It makes security levels and restrictions highly configurable and extends them beyond applets. With Java 2, any Java code, whether it is an applet, a servlet, a JavaBeans component, or a complete Java application, can be run with restricted permissions that prevent it from doing harm to the host system.

The security features of the Java language and the Java platform have been subjected to intense scrutiny by security experts around the world. Security-related bugs, some of them potentially serious, have been found and fixed. The new security model will probably also have bugs in it, and these will, over time, be found and fixed as well.

Because of the security promises Java makes, it is big news when a new security bug is found. Remember, however, that no other mainstream platform can make security guarantees nearly as strong as those that Java makes. If Java's security is not yet perfect, it is has been proven strong enough for practical day-to-day use, and is certainly better than any of the alternatives.

Network-centric Programming

Sun's corporate motto has always been "The network is the computer." The designers of the Java platform believed in the importance of networking and designed the Java platform to be network-centric. From a programmer's point of view, Java makes it unbelievably easy to work with resources across a network and to create network-based applications using client/server or multi-tier architectures. This means that Java programmers have a serious head start in the emerging network economy.

Dynamic, Extensible Programs

Java is both dynamic and extensible. Java code is organized into modular object-oriented units called *classes*. Classes are stored in separate files and are loaded into the Java interpreter only when needed. This means that an application can decide as it is running what classes it needs, and can load them when it needs them. In also means that a program can dynamically extend itself by loading the classes it needs to expand its functionality.

The network-centric design of the Java platform means that a Java application can dynamically extend itself by loading new classes over a network. An application that takes advantage of these features ceases to be a monolithic block of code. Instead, it becomes an interacting collection of independent software components. Thus, Java enables a powerful new metaphor of application design and development.

Internationalization

The Java language and the Java platform were designed from the start with the rest of the world in mind. Java is the only commonly used programming language that has internationalization features at its very core, rather than tacked on as an afterthought. While most programming languages use 8-bit characters that can represent only the alphabets of English and Western European languages, Java uses 16-bit Unicode characters that represent the phonetic alphabets and ideographic character sets of the entire world. In addition, Java's internationalization features are not restricted to just low-level character representation. These features permeate the Java platform, making it easier to write internationalized programs with Java than it is with any other environment.

Performance

Programs written in Java are compiled to a portable, intermediate-form known as "byte code", rather than to native machine language instructions. The Java Virtual Machine runs a Java program by interpreting these portable byte-code instructions. This architecture means that Java programs are faster than programs or scripts written in purely interpreted languages, but they are typically slower than C and C++ programs that are compiled to native machine language. Remember, however, that although Java programs are compiled to byte code, not all of the Java platform is implemented with interpreted byte codes. For efficiency, computationally-intensive portions of the Java platform—such as the string manipulation methods—are implemented using native machine code.

Although early releases of Java suffered from performance problems, the speed of the Java VM has improved dramatically with each new release. The VM has been higly tuned and optimized in many significant ways. Furthermore, many implementations include a just-in-time compiler, which converts Java byte codes to native machine instructions on the fly. Sun is even planning to sell a VM implementation using what they call "hot spot" technology: it performs selective just-in-time compilation only for pieces of code that are frequently executed. The result, they claim, is Java applications that execute at the speed of native C and C++ applications.

Java is a portable, interpreted language; Java programs run almost as fast as native, non-portable C and C++ programs. Performance used to be an issue that made some programmers avoid using Java. Now, with the improvements made in Java 2, performance issues should no longer keep anyone away. In fact, the winning combination of performance plus portability is a unique feature that no other language can offer.

Programmer Efficiency and Time-to-Market

The final, and perhaps most important, reason to use Java is that programmers like it. Java is an elegant language combined with a powerful and well-designed set of APIs. Programmers enjoy programming in Java, and are usually amazed at how quickly they can get results with it. Studies have shown consistently that switching to Java increases programmer efficiency. Because Java is a simple and elegant language with a well-designed, intuitive set of APIs, programmers write better code with fewer bugs than they do for other platforms, again reducing development time.

Java 2 or Java 1.2?

The announcement of the Java 2 platform caught the community of Java developers by surprise. Throughout nearly a year of beta-testing, the release had been called "Java 1.2." Then, just as the final code was released, the name was changed from "Java 1.2" to "the Java 2 platform."

This was a marketing ploy, of course. But, in addition to its marketing benefits, the name change accurately reflects the true state of the Java platform. As I noted at the beginning of this chapter, this latest release is three times as large as the Java 1.1 release and seven times as large as the original Java 1.0 release. And that's before counting the important standard extensions that are an optional part of the Java platform.

But the change is not just a quantitative one. It is highly qualitative as well. The new release provides crucial graphics and user interface features, and fills in a number of previously missing pieces. Java 2 is the first release of Java that truly defines a complete, mature, and robust platform for developers to target. It is these qualitative changes, more than the mere size increase, that justify the jump to Java 2.

With that said, note that there is bound to be confusion about the version number. As I write this, the Java interpreter supplied with the Java 2 platform reports a version number of 1.2. I imagine that the release engineers at Sun are really, really annoyed with the marketing folks who changed the number at the last minute. Right now, it has not become clear how this version number incompatibility will be resolved. The phrase "Java 2 platform" refers to the Java specification. It may be that the terms "Java 1.2" and "JDK 1.2" will continue to be used to refer to Sun's implementation of that platform.

With that matter of nomenclature behind us, let's proceed to explore the features and capabilities of the Java 2 platform.

Core Features of Java 2

The Java platform provides all the core features that you'd expect to find in any programming environment. The difference between Java and other platforms is that the core Java APIs are object-oriented and exceptionally well designed. The elegance of the core features makes Java programming easier and more efficient. The following sections highlight the most important core features of the Java platform.

Language Fundamentals

As I already mentioned, the Java platform is made up of modular object-oriented units known as classes. Related classes are grouped into packages. The java.lang package contains the classes that are most fundamental to the Java platform and the Java programming language. It contains classes that represent strings of text, threads of execution, exceptions, and errors. Other classes in java.lang are fundamental to the dynamic class loading and security protection mechanisms of Java.

java.lang and a related package, java.lang.reflect, contain classes that support introspection, allowing a Java program to reflect upon itself. The classes represent Java packages, Java classes, and the methods and fields of Java classes. With these classes, a Java program can find out about the methods of a particular object, for example. Introspection is particularly useful for creating scripting languages and visual programming tools that dynamically manipulate Java objects.

Input/Output

The java.io package contains classes for performing input and output. The basic abstraction of the Java I/O system is a sequential stream of bytes or characters. The majority of the classes in this package represent and manipulate streams of bytes or characters. Java streams gain much of their power from their ability to be flexibly combined. For example, FileInputStream is a low-level class that reads bytes from a file (assuming, of course, that the program is not subject to security restrictions that prevent it from reading files). An InputStreamReader reads bytes from a byte stream, such as a FileInputStream, and converts the stream of bytes to a stream of characters. A BufferedReader reads characters in bulk from a character stream, such as an InputStreamReader, and buffers them up for more efficient use later. A Java program can combine these three modular stream classes to read text from a file in an efficient manner.

The java.io package contains numerous stream classes. There are classes that read data from files and write data to files. There are also classes that allow character stream and byte stream input to and output from strings and arrays. Other classes support pipes that transfer data to and from other threads in the same program.

Some of the most exciting capabilities of streams occur in conjunction with the networking capabilities of the java.net package (covered in the next section). The Java stream abstraction allows streams of bytes and characters to be read from and written to the network as easily as they can be read from and written to files on the local hard disk.

Another important feature of the java.io package is the ability to *serialize* a Java object into a stream of bytes that can be stored in a file or transferred across a network. Serialization is supported by the ObjectInputStream and ObjectOutputStream classes. The ObjectOutputStream serializes a Java object, while the ObjectInputStream does the opposite, reading a stream of bytes from a file, network, or other source and converting the data back into the Java object that it represents. This is a tremendously powerful capability in any object-oriented system, and is particularly useful for networked, object-oriented enterprise software.

The input/output capabilities of Java are not restricted entirely to streams of bytes and characters, however. The File class represents files and directories in the local file system and allows manipulation of those files and directories. The RandomAccessFile class allows random access to files, as an alternative to the sequential access allowed by the stream classes.

Two utility packages also provide important input/output capabilities. java.util.zip contains classes for compressing and decompressing arbitrary streams of data and for reading and writing compressed files in ZIP and GZIP format. java.util.jar contains classes that support the JAR (Java Archive) file format.

For complete coverage of all the I/O classes available in Java, see *Java I/O* by Elliotte Rusty Harold (O'Reilly).

Networking

Programming languages and operating system platforms that evolved before the advent of the Internet and the ubiquity of networking typically have networking capabilities tacked on in an awkward way. Networking APIs on these platforms are usually poorly documented, and are considered arcane, wizard-level stuff. Not so with Java. Networking is a central feature of the Java platform; the networking APIs were designed to be as easy to use as any other part of the system.

Java networking classes are grouped in the java.net package. At the highest level, the Java platform supports networking through Internet URLs. By default, the platform supports HTTP, FTP, and local file URLs, and can be dynamically extended to support URLs that use other Internet protocols. The URL class represents an arbitrary URL and can open a stream to the network resource it refers to, so that a Java program can read or write binary data or text from or to any network resource that can be identified with a URL.

At a slightly lower level, the Socket class represents a network connection to another computer. The Socket class also works with the classes in the java.io package to allow stream-based exchange of data between computers on the network. The Socket class is used by both client and server programs. In addition, the ServerSocket class provides a kind of network doorbell for servers: it allows servers to listen for and accept connection requests from clients.

The java.net package provides an even lower level of networking support through the DatagramPacket and DatagramSocket classes. These allow a Java program to send or receive packets of data across the network. Instead of allowing stream-based exchange of data, these classes allow very efficient transmission of single blocks of binary data.

Like all resource-sensitive features of Java, access to networking capabilities is protected by the Java security mechanisms. Java code cannot talk to other computers unless it is explicitly granted permission to do so. By default, untrusted code is granted very limited networking permissions.

Java networking capabilities are covered in much greater detail in *Java Network Programming* by Elliotte Rusty Harold (O'Reilly).

Math

The java.lang.Math class provides floating point mathematics capabilities for the Java platform. This class defines important numeric constants such as e and π and methods that perform trigonometric, logarithmic, and other mathematical operations.

The java.math package contains classes that support arbitrary-precision arithmetic on integers and floating-point numbers.

Data Structures and Utilities

The java.util package contains, as the name implies, a number of utility classes. Most important among these are the collections classes introduced with the Java 2 platform. The collection classes provide predefined, efficient, throughly tested implementations of data structures and algorithms for dealing with collections of objects. These predefined collections and the algorithms that sort, search, and perform other manipulations on them make it easier to develop and maintain Java programs that are less prone to bugs and more efficient and reliable.

The java.util package also contains a number of other miscellaneous utility classes. These include classes for working with dates, times, and time zones; a class for generating random numbers; a class for representing an internationalization locale; and a class for performing simple parsing of strings.

Internationalization

The java.text package contains classes that support the internationalization and localization of Java programs, so that they can run in any locale in the world. These classes are primarily concerned with the correct representation and manipulation of text in international and multilingual environments. The package also includes classes that display numbers, dates, and currency values according to the the accepted conventions of a given locale. In Java 2, the internationalization capabilities have even been extended to handle the complex details of bidirectional text, as used in Hebrew and Arabic.

Security

Security mechanisms are found throughout the Java language, the Java interpreter, and the Java platform. Prior to the Java 2 platform, the `SecurityManager` and `ClassLoader` classes in the `java.lang` package were the main security mechanisms in Java. Now, some of the most important mechanisms are part of the `java.security` package.

The `Permission` class represents a permission granted to a particular piece of Java code. Numerous subclasses of this class are found throughout other packages of the Java platform. These subclasses represent specific types of permissions, such as the permission to read or write a file, the permission to network with another computer, the permission to start a print job, and so forth.

The `Policy` class represents a security policy for the Java environment. The details of a security policy are configurable, at a fine-grained level, by the end user or system administrator. A security policy might grant no permissions to Java code downloaded across the network, while granting numerous sensitive permissions to trusted Java applications that are installed locally. However, the same policy might restrict the permissions that are available to the JavaBeans components that are dynamically loaded by the trusted application.

The `java.security` package and its subpackages also include classes that use the techniques of public key cryptography to generate and manipulate public and private keys and key certificates. These packages define classes for creating digital signatures based on public key cryptography, for computing cryptographically secure message digests for arbitrary data, and for defining and manipulating access control lists.

However, because of restrictive U.S. export regulations, the `java.security` packages stop just short of providing actual data encryption and decryption capabilities. Encryption and decryption fall within the domain of the Java Cryptography Extension, or JCE, which is available as a standard extension. Sun's implementation of the JCE is available only within the U.S. and Canada, but other implementations developed in other countries—and therefore exempt from the U.S. export regulations—will presumably become available.

For a complete discussion of the security features in Java, see *Java Security*, by Scott Oaks (O'Reilly). *Java Cryptography*, by Jonathan Knudsen (O'Reilly), delves into the details of cryptography as it relates to Java programming.

User Interface Features

Graphical user interfaces (GUIs) were a weak spot of the initial releases of Java. Java 1.0 and Java 1.1 provided a user-interface library called the Abstract Windowing Toolkit (AWT) that was layered on top of platform-native GUI components.

The task of layering a platform-independent GUI toolkit on top of multiple divergent native GUI toolkits proved to be exceedingly complex. The approach also meant that the Java GUI system was restricted to the lowest common denominator functionality of the various native toolkits. The result was a crippled GUI system; it was nearly impossible to create GUIs with Java that could compete with the GUIs of native applications.

The Java 2 platform solves these problems by abandoning the previous approach and implementing a pure-Java, cross-platform GUI library from scratch.* This library, commonly called "Swing," is as powerful and full-featured as any native GUI system in existence. Swing, along with Java 2D, is part of the Java Foundation Classes, or JFC. In addition to a full set of JavaBeans-compatible GUI components, Swing and the JFC define a number of application services that create a full-featured and robust framework within which GUI applications can be developed.

The following sections provide an overview of the GUI and application services features of Swing and the JFC.

Swing Components

The most visible and important part of any GUI library is the set of GUI components it provides. Swing provides a full and powerful set, summarized in Table 1-1. This set of components is impressive in its own right. It is even more impressive when you realize that each component is also a JavaBeans component, that each component offers a pluggable look-and-feel that can be configured dynamically, and that each component supports the Accessibility API (described later in this chapter) to enable assistive technologies for disabled users.

The Swing components require no further introduction. If you read through the table, they speak for themselves. Remember that although the GUI components are the most visible part of Swing, they are only a part of it. Other parts of Swing, described later in this section, provide an application framework and application services. For more complete coverage of Swing, see *Java Swing*, by Robert Eckstein, Marc Loy, and Dave Wood (O'Reilly).

The Swing components are contained in a package named javax.swing. "javax" in a package name usually indicates that the package is a standard extension. Don't let this name confuse you. Swing was an extension to Java 1.1, but it is a very important core part of Java 2.

Table 1-1: GUI Components of Swing

Component Name	Description
Box	A general-purpose container that arranges children using the model of BoxLayout.
JApplet	An Applet subclass containing a JRootPane to add Swing features, such as support for menubars.
JButton	A push button that can display text, images, or both.

---

* Java 2 retains backward compatibility with previous releases, of course.

Table 1-1: GUI Components of Swing (continued)

Component Name	Description
JCheckBox	A toggle button for displaying choices that are not mutually exclusive.
JCheckBoxMenuItem	A check box designed for use in menus.
JColorChooser	A complex, customizable component that allows the user to select a color from one or more color spaces. Used in conjunction with the `javax.swing.color-chooser` package.
JComboBox	A combination of a text entry field and a drop-down list of choices. The user can type a selection or choose one from the list.
JComponent	The root of the Swing component hierarchy. Adds Swing-specific features such as tooltips and support for double-buffering.
JDesktopPane	A container for `JInternalFrame` components; simulates the operation of a desktop within a single window. Supports MDI (multiple document interface) application styles.
JDialog	The container used to display dialog boxes in Swing.
JEditorPane	A powerful text editor, customizable via an `EditorKit` object. Predefined editor kits exist for displaying and editing HTML and RTF-format text.
JFileChooser	A complex component that allows the user to select a file or directory. Supports filtering and optional file previews. Used in conjunction with the `javax.swing.filechooser` package.
JFrame	The container used for top-level windows in Swing.
JInternalFrame	A lightweight nested window container. Behaves like a `JFrame` and displays a titlebar and resize handles, but is not an independent window, and is constrained to appear within the bounds of its parent container. Often used with `JDesktopPane`.
JLabel	A simple component that displays text, an image, or both. Does not respond to input.
JLayeredPane	A container that allows its children to overlap. Manages the stacking order of those children.
JList	A component that displays a selectable list of choices. The choices are usually strings or images, but arbitrary objects may also be displayed.

Table 1-1: GUI Components of Swing (continued)

Component Name	Description
JMenu	A pulldown menu in a JMenuBar, or a submenu within another menu.
JMenuBar	A component that displays a set of pulldown menus.
JMenuItem	A selectable item within a menu.
JOptionPane	A complex component suitable for displaying simple dialogs within a JDialog container. Defines useful static methods for displaying common dialog types.
JPanel	A generic container for grouping components with an appropriate LayoutManager.
JPasswordField	A text input field for sensitive data, such as passwords. For security, does not display the text as it is typed.
JPopupMenu	A window that pops up to display a menu. Used by JMenu and for standalone popup menus.
JProgressBar	A component that displays the progress of a time-consuming operation.
JRadioButton	A toggle button for displaying mutually exclusive choices.
JRadioButtonMenuItem	A radio button for use in menus.
JRootPane	A complex container used internally by JApplet, JDialog, JFrame, and JInternalFrame. Provides a number of important Swing capabilities to the containers that use it.
JScrollBar	A horizontal or vertical scrollbar.
JScrollPane	A container that allows a child component to be scrolled horizontally or vertically. Supports scrolling and non-scrolling header regions at the top and left of the scrolling region.
JSeparator	A simple component that draws a horizontal or vertical line. Used to visually divide complex interfaces into sections.
JSlider	A component that simulates a slider control like those found on stereo equalizers. Allows the user to select a numeric value by dragging a knob. Can display tick marks and labels.
JSplitPane	A container that displays two children by splitting itself horizontally or vertically. Allows the user to adjust the amount of space allocated to each child.

Table 1-1: GUI Components of Swing (continued)

Component Name	Description
JTabbedPane	A container that displays one child at a time, allowing the user to select the currently displayed child by clicking on tabs like those found on manila file folders.
JTable	A complex and powerful component for displaying tables and editing their contents. Typically used to display strings, but may be customized to display any type of data. Used in conjunction with the javax.swing.table package.
JTextArea	A component for displaying and editing multiple lines of plain text. Based on JTextComponent.
JTextComponent	The root component of a powerful and highly customizable text display and editing system. Part of the javax.swing.text package.
JTextField	A component for the display, input, and editing of a single line of plain text. Based on JTextComponent.
JTextPane	A subclass of JEditorPane for displaying and editing formatted text that is not in HTML or RTF format. Suitable for adding simple word processing functionality to an application.
JToggleButton	The parent component of both JCheckBox and JRadioButton.
JToolBar	A component that displays a set of user-selectable tools or actions.
JToolTip	A lightweight popup window that displays simple documentation or tips when the mouse pointer lingers over a component.
JTree	A powerful component for the display of tree-structured data. Data values are typically strings, but the component can be customized to display any kind of data. Used in conjunction with the javax.swing.tree package.
JViewport	A fixed-size container that displays a portion of a larger child. Usually used as part of a JScrollPane.
JWindow	A top-level Swing window that does not display a titlebar, resize handles, or any other decorations.

Model/View Separation

Swing is based on a model/view architecture that separates component state from the object that displays and allows the user to interact with that state. Every Swing component that has state (for example, the currently selected item in a JList) maintains that state in a separate object known as its *model*. Swing includes interfaces that define the state maintained by each model and provides default implementations of those interfaces.

Separating model objects from the components has two important benefits. First, it allows multiple components to share a model object and provide different views of the model. Second, it allows application data structures to be defined in such a way that they implement one or more model interfaces. This allows those application-specific data structures to be displayed directly by Swing components. For example, a data structure that represents tree-structured data can implement the TreeModel interface, automatically allowing it to be displayed in a JTree object.

Pluggable Look-and-Feel

We've already seen that Swing components use a model/view architecture and the model is a separate object from the component itself. As it turns out, the view is also separate from the component. This leaves the component with the task of handling the interaction between the model and the view. The view object is known as the UI delegate; its job is to display the component and handle input from the user. In other words, the UI delegate is responsible for the look-and-feel of a component.

An important feature of Swing is its pluggable look-and-feel architecture. An application or an end user can specify a desired look-and-feel. When Swing components are created, their UI delegate objects are selected based on the requested look-and-feel. This allows complete customization of the appearance and behavior of any Swing application. Swing ships with a default Java look-and-feel (also known as the Metal look-and-feel), as well as implementations that mimic the look-and-feel of both Motif and Windows. A Macintosh-based look-and-feel implementation is available separately. Thus, any Swing application can have the distinctive appearance of a Java application or the familiar appearance of a platform-native application. Figure 1-1 shows examples of the Metal, Motif, and Windows look-and-feels.

Accessibility

The Java 2 platform includes the new javax.accessibility package as part of the JFC. This package defines classes that are used by assistive technologies to make applications more accessible to disabled people. For example, a blind person might use a screen reader as an assistive technology.

All Swing components are accessible, which means that they implement standard methods that assistive technologies can query to obtain information about individual components. Thus, when you create an application using Swing components,

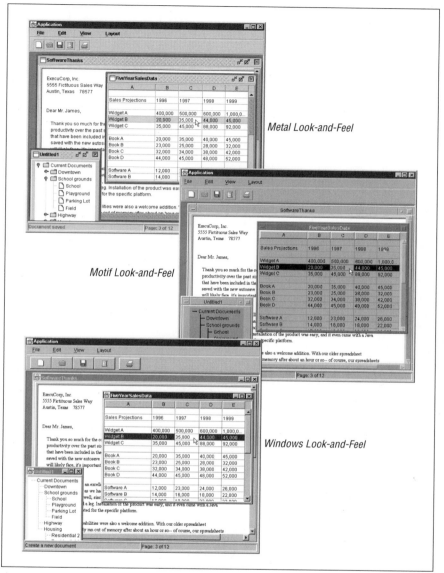

Figure 1-1: Various look-and-feels for Swing components

your application is automatically accessible. This brings your application to a large audience of users who would not be able to use it otherwise, and it requires no extra programming effort on your part.

Miscellaneous Swing Features

There are a number of miscellaneous features of Swing that are important and useful enough to warrant a mention in this overview:

Borders

Every Swing component can have a Border object displayed around it. The javax.swing.border package defines a number of commonly used border types, such as beveled, grooved, and titled borders.

Tooltips

Swing supports context-sensitive help through *tooltips* (small boxes of text that pop up when the mouse lingers over a component). Swing handles the creation and display of tooltips automatically; all you have to do is supply appropriate text for the tips.

Actions

GUI applications often allow a user to invoke an operation in a number of different ways. For example, the user may be able to save a file by either selecting an item from a menu or clicking on a button in a toolbar. The resulting operation is exactly the same; it is simply presented to the user through two different interfaces.

Swing defines a simple but powerful interface named Action, which encapsulates information about such an operation. An Action object includes the method that performs the desired operation, a short string of text that names the operation, an image that can be used to represent the action graphically, and a longer string of text suitable for use in a tooltip for the action.

You can add an Action object directly to JMenu and JToolBar components. This makes the action's operation available to the user, displaying the action's textual description and graphical image as appropriate. Action objects can be enabled
and disabled. When an action is disabled, any component that presents the action to the user does not allow the user to select or invoke it.

In this way, the Action interface helps Swing programmers implement a very clean separation between GUI code and application logic.

Timers

The Java platform makes it very easy to work with multiple threads. To perform a repetitive or delayed action, such as animation, in Java, it is common to create a new thread that spends most of its time waiting for time to pass. While it is relatively easy to do this in Java, it is not as easy as it should be. To make it even easier, Swing includes a new Timer class that automatically triggers a single or periodic event after a specified period of time. Although conceptually simple, timers are an integral part of the complete Swing application framework and are a powerful service available to all Swing applications.

Undo Framework

The javax.swing.undo package provides a standard, general-purpose framework for implementing **Undo** and **Redo** operations in Swing applications. The framework centers around a list of UndoableEdit objects that describe recent changes made in the application and allow those changes to be undone. Note that this framework is not limited to text editing changes; it can be used for any kind of change to an application. While this framework does not automate undo and redo processing for Swing applications, it simplifies these operations considerably.

Mouseless Operation

The Swing components and their pluggable look-and-feel implementations were designed to work with Swing's powerful keyboard navigation (or keyboard traversal) mechanism. All of the standard Swing components can be operated entirely from the keyboard without the use of the mouse. This is a very desirable feature, especially for advanced users.

Drag-and-Drop

The Java 2 platform allows Java applications to interact with native applications through drag-and-drop. This is a feature that was sorely missing from previous Java releases. Java 1.0 had no data-transfer capabilities. Java 1.1 introduced rudimentary cut and paste capabilities, but did not support drag-and-drop.

The drag-and-drop implementation in the Java 2 platform is full-featured. For example, it includes the ability to perform drag-over and drag-under animations. Furthermore, access to the drag-and-drop system is controlled by the Java security mechanisms. This prevents untrusted code from gaining access to sensitive data that is accidentally or unknowingly dropped on its user interface. Drag-and-drop is implemented in the java.awt.dnd package.

Input Method Support

An *input method* is a program that allows a user to enter text in an ideographic language such as Chinese or Japanese using a keyboard with a relatively small number of keys. Since words in these languages are represented as single characters, there are a vast number of possible characters, and entering a character usually requires several keystrokes. An input method operates in conjunction with an external dictionary to convert sequences of keystrokes into the desired ideographic character.

Support for input methods is required for any computer system to be used in a country that does not use a phonetic alphabet. Previous releases of Java could be customized to work with input methods, but the Java 2 platform now delivers input method support as a core part of the platform. The input method framework is defined in the java.awt.im package. The framework also relies on some of the internationalization classes in java.text. Swing text input components are implemented to support the input method framework, so they interact well with input methods.

Note that the concept of an input method can be generalized beyond its traditional use for input of ideographic characters. A speech recognition system, for example, could be implemented as an input method. Such an input method could be automatically plugged into any Swing application so that the application could accept spoken input instead of typed input. Considered in this light, input methods are another piece of the accessibility framework.

JavaHelp

JavaHelp is a standard extension to Java 2 that is implemented in the `javax.javahelp` package and its subpackages. JavaHelp provides a framework for defining and displaying online help in Java applications and applets. JavaHelp uses Swing components (and defines some of its own) to be able to display both an expandable, tree-structured table of contents and hyperlinked, formatted text.

Applets

No discussion of the user-interface capabilities of the Java platform would be complete without a discussion of applets. As the name implies, an applet is a mini-application. Specifically, it is a Java program designed to be downloaded across a network and executed within a web browser. Because they are loaded across an open network, applets are typically considered untrusted code and are run with a full complement of security restrictions, to prevent them from doing any damage to the local system.

Applets popularized the initial release of Java, and they have changed little since Java 1.0. Java 2 enhances applets with the Swing `JApplet` class and its new, more flexible security model.

Both the base `Applet` class and the Swing `JApplet` extension of that class are GUI containers that can hold other GUI components and containers. Thus, a discussion of applets is appropriate in this discussion of GUI features of Java. However, the compelling features of applets are not their user-interface capabilities. What makes applets interesting is exactly what makes the Java platform interesting: they are network-centric, dynamically extensible, and secure.

JavaBeans

Just as no discussion of GUIs in Java is complete without a mention of applets, no discussion of GUI components is complete without a mention of JavaBeans. If applets were one of the most exciting features of Java 1.0, beans were one of the most exciting features of Java 1.1. Support for beans is extended in the Java 2 platform.

JavaBeans is the Java component system. A bean is a Java object whose API follows certain conventions. These conventions allow the bean to be manipulated by various tools, such as visual application builder tools. The conventions also allow scripting languages to manipulate beans easily. To a certain extent, the conventions even allow an application to be assembled dynamically as a group of independent but interacting beans. Beans are usually, but not always, GUI components. All of the GUI components defined by the Java platform follow the JavaBeans conventions and therefore can be used as beans. A bean can be as simple as a push button or as complex as a full-featured word processor. For complete information on JavaBeans, see *Developing Java Beans*, by Robert Englander (O'Reilly).

Prior to Java 2, an application could be created as a collection of beans, but there was no way to nest beans. The Java 2 platform defines the notion of a *bean context*: a container that can hold beans and other bean contexts. A bean context may also provide a set of services—such as the ability to print—to the beans it contains. In some ways, this is an extension of the applet model: a bean context is to a bean as a web browser is to an applet. In fact, the Java 2 platform provides support for objects that can be used interchangeably as beans or applets.

The new drag-and-drop features of the Java 2 platform are particularly important for the JavaBeans component model. Drag-and-drop provides a user-driven mechanism for transferring data between independent modular beans that operate as part of the same application but know nothing about each other.

The Java 2 platform includes a standard extension known as the Java Activation Framework, or JAF. This extension is in essence a JavaBeans component registry. For any given data type (any MIME type), this registry maintains a list of beans available on the system that can operate in some way (e.g., display, edit, print) on that data.

When an application needs to operate on data of a given type, it can use the JAF to obtain dynamically a list of operations that are supported on the current system for that type of data. If the application finds the operation it wants, it can use the JAF to instantiate an appropriate bean and associate the data with it. Then, the application can use the bean to perform the desired operation. The JAF is defined in the javax.activation package.

There's yet another standard extension to the Java 2 platform that falls loosely within the domain of JavaBeans. The InfoBus API, implemented in the javax.infobus package, provides a mechanism for data exchange between beans or between any group of objects. The infobus architecture is modeled on the notion of a bus in computer hardware: any number of beans can plug into an infobus to share data, just as any number of computer peripherals can plug into a computer's bus.

Graphics Features

Prior to Java 2, graphics was another of the weak areas of the Java platform. Previous versions supported simple text rendering, line drawing, area filling, and image display functions, but these features were primitive at best, largely because of the challenges of providing complex graphics capabilities in a platform-independent way. Printing support was nonexistent in Java 1.0 and rudimentary in Java 1.1.

With the Java 2 platform, it is an entirely different story. Java 2 provides powerful, state-of-the-art two-dimensional graphics capabilities and, as a standard extension, high-quality three-dimensional graphics capabilities. Also, support for colors, fonts, image manipulation, and printing is greatly improved with Java 2. Another standard extension, the Java Media Framework, adds audio and video multimedia capabilities. The sections that follow provide an overview of the graphics features of the Java 2 platform.

Java 2D

Java 2D is a powerful new graphics model defined by Sun and various industry partners. Programmers who have worked with the PostScript or Display PostScript page description languages should find many of its concepts familiar. The classes for Java 2D are in the java.awt package and its subpackages. For a complete discussion of Java 2D, see *Java 2D Graphics*, by Jonathan Knudsen (O'Reilly).

The Java 2D graphics model allows you to define and manipulate arbitrary Shape objects. Shapes can be stroked (outlined) using lines of any width, color, dash pattern, and join style, and they can be filled with any color, color gradient, or pattern. There are methods to transform shapes and images by translation, rotation, scaling, flipping, and skewing. The entire coordinate system used for drawing can also be transformed by any of these methods. You can take advantage of powerful color compositing and alpha transparency features to blend colors and make shapes and images appear partially transparent. All Java 2D drawing may be done directly on screen or into an offscreen image.

Java 2D also allows you to do sophisticated things with text. Text of any size can be drawn using any font available on the system. You can treat individual glyphs of a font as individual shapes, so they can be arbitrarily stroked, filled, transformed, and composited. Text, or any shape, can be rendered using automatic anti-aliasing, if desired.

Java 2D shapes can distinguish their inside from their outside, which means they can be used to define arbitrary clipping regions and perform hit detection for mouse clicks. Java 2D includes a number of classes that represent commonly used shapes, and allows arbitrary shapes and curves to be defined out of line segments and Bézier curves. It also allows shapes to be combined through addition, intersection, and subtraction to produce compound shapes.

Figure 1-2 shows some of capabilities of Java 2D.

Color

Java 2D defines a ColorSpace object that supports arbitrary color spaces. It defines mechanisms for converting colors from any one color space to any other color space, including the standard RGB color space. It also supports international standards for the specification of device-independent color. The java.awt.color package contains classes that implement color handling, but most applications should not need to use these classes. Instead, use the java.awt.Color class, which has been modified to support the new color functionality.

Fonts

The earlier releases of Java supported only a handful of supposedly platform-independent fonts. The Java 2 platform, through Java 2D, can now use any font installed on the host system. This is a substantial step forward, and will go a long way towards improving the graphic design of Java applications. As with color, the low-level implementation of fonts is provided in a subpackage, the java.awt.font package. You don't have to use the classes in this package to take advantage of the new font features. Instead, you can rely on the higher-level text display

Figure 1-2: Java 2D demonstration

features of java.awt and javax.swing. You can also use the java.awt.Font class, which has been modified to support the new features.

Mouse pointers

In Java 1.0, an application could choose one of 14 predefined mouse pointers for each window it displayed. With Java 1.1, each component could have its own pointer, but could still only choose from 14 predefined ones. This arbitrary restriction has been lifted by the Java 2 platform. An application can now use any small image as a mouse pointer.

Image processing

The image-processing model of the initial releases of Java was optimized for use with images downloaded over a slow network. At best, the model was confusing and difficult to use. The Java 2 platform includes a new image-processing model as part of Java 2D. This model is compatible with the Java 1.0 APIs, but works well with images that are resident in memory. It includes powerful image filters that can perform common image-processing tasks. The Java 2D image-processing model is implemented by classes in the java.awt.image package.

Printing

Java 1.0 had no printing capabilities at all. Java 1.1 had rudimentary capabilities that did not interact well with the native printing systems on various platforms. For example, it did not bring up the standard **Print** dialog box on Windows systems. The Java 2 platform includes full-featured printing capabilities as part of Java 2D in the `java.awt.print` package. The printing API supports single-page and multi-page documents, as well as variable page and margins sizes. These new printing capabilities interact well with the native printing systems on host computers.

Java 3D

Just as Java 2D brings state-of-the-art two-dimensional graphics to the Java 2 platform, the Java 3D API brings powerful state-of-the-art three-dimensional graphics capabilities to the platform. Unlike Java 2D, however, the Java 3D API is a standard extension to the Java platform, defined in the `javax.media.j3d` package. This means that it is not guaranteed to be available on every Java installation. Figure 1-3 shows some of the capabilities of Java 3D.

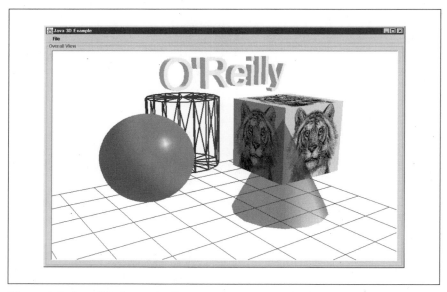

Figure 1-3: Java 3D demonstration

The designers of Java 3D studied existing 3D graphics systems, such as OpenGL, Direct3D, and QuickDraw3D, and picked the best features of each to create a powerful, high-level API. Programming with Java 3D involves a number of steps. First, the three-dimensional geometry of each object to be rendered is defined. This can be done by a program, or the geometry data can be read in from a file or network using an existing data format, such as that used by a CAD program or VRML. The next step is to place the virtual objects into a virtual world by linking their geometry descriptions into a tree structure called a scene graph. Next, rendering attributes such as lighting and viewing angle are defined. Finally, the virtual world is drawn, using one of three possible rendering modes, each of which has different tradeoffs between flexibility and efficiency.

In addition to three-dimensional graphics, Java 3D also provides classes to describe and play "three-dimensional" sounds, a powerful capability that is useful in virtual reality and immersive game environments. The javax.vecmath package is an auxiliary API that is part of the Java 3D framework. This package contains classes that perform the vector and matrix arithmetic required for 3D graphics.

Java Media Framework

The Java Media Framework, or JMF, is another standard extension to the Java 2 platform. It defines a framework for working with time-based media such as audio and video. In addition to its capabilities for playing audio data and displaying video data encoded in a wide variety of formats, JMF includes features for processing, controlling, and synchronizing streams of multimedia data. JMF works with data stored locally in files and with compressed streaming data delivered in real time across a network.

A pure-Java implementation of JMF is available for use on any Java platform. In addition, there are OS-specific implementations that use native code to increase performance and support media formats that are not practical in the pure-Java version.

Future versions of JMF will also include capabilities for media capture (recording) and conferencing.

Sound

The first two releases of Java supported only very rudimentary sound capabilities. Only sounds encoded in Sun's AU format could be played. The API was such that only applets, not applications, could easily play sounds.

The implementation of the Java 2 platform includes a new sound engine that supports a complete set of commonly used audio file formats. In addition, there have been API changes that allow sounds to be played by any Java code, not just applets. Note also that the JMF handles a wide variety of sound formats.

The sound engine included in the core Java 2 platform can be controlled using the new Java Sound API, a standard extension that is under development as of this writing. While the current core APIs support the playing of simple sounds, Java Sound will offer complete audio control.

Enterprise Features

The largest and most visible new features of the Java 2 platform are in the area of graphical user interfaces and graphics. The most strategically important features, however, may be the Java Enterprise APIs. These are APIs that allow Java to be used for mission critical business applications that must run in large, heterogenous, networked environments that include legacy systems.

Some of the Java Enterprise APIs were available in Java 1.1, while others are new in Java 2. Some are core APIs, while others are standard extensions. Still, the Enterprise APIs stand out in the Java 2 platform because, for the first time, the Java platform offers a complete, mature set of APIs for enterprise applications.

The sections that follow briefly describe each of the Enterprise APIs found in the Java 2 platform.

Database Access

The Java Database Connectivity (JDBC) API allows a Java program to send SQL query and update statements to a database server and to retrieve and iterate through query results returned by the server. JDBC also allows you to get meta-information about the database and its tables from the database server. The JDBC architecture relies upon a Driver class that hides the details of communicating with a database server. Each database server product requires a custom Driver implementation so that Java programs can communicate with it. Major database vendors have made JDBC drivers available for their products. In addition, a "bridge" driver exists to enable Java programs to communicate with databases through existing ODBC drivers.

The JDBC API is found in the java.sql package, which was introduced in Java 1.1. The Java 2 platform adds a number of new classes to this package to support advanced database features. Java 2 also adds additional features in the javax.sql standard extension package. javax.sql provides features for treating database query results as JavaBeans, for pooling database connections, and for obtaining database connection information from a name service.

The JDBC API is simple and well-designed. Programmers who are familiar with SQL and database programming in general should find it very easy to work with databases in Java. For more details about JDBC, see *Database Programming with JDBC and Java*, by George Reese (O'Reilly).

Distributed Objects with RMI

Distributed objects offer a powerful model for object-oriented network programming that has become quite popular in recent years. This model holds that a client should be able to invoke methods of remote server objects as if those remote objects existed locally on the client. This general model can be implemented in a number of ways. One of those ways is the Java Remote Method Invocation (RMI) API. RMI is implemented in the java.rmi package, which was introduced in Java 1.1 and has been enhanced for the Java 2 platform.

The Java RMI implementation is full-featured, but still simple and easy to use. It gains much of its simplicity by being built on top of a network-centric and dynamically extensible platform, of course. But it also gains simplicity by requiring both client and server to be implemented in Java. This requirement ensures that both client and server share a common set of data types and have access to the object serialization and deserialization features of the java.io package, for example. On the other hand, this means that RMI cannot be used with distributed objects written in languages other than Java, such as objects that exist on legacy servers. It also means that servers written using RMI can be used only by clients written in

Java. In practice, RMI is an excellent distributed object solution for situations where it is clear that clients and servers will always be written in Java. Fortunately, there are many such situations.

The `java.rmi` package makes it easy to create networked, object-oriented programs. Programmers who have spent time writing networked applications using lower-level technologies are usually amazed by the power of RMI. By making RMI so easy, `java.rmi` points the way to future applications and systems that consist of loose groups of objects interacting with each other over a network, These objects may act both as clients, by calling methods of other objects, and as servers, by exposing their own methods to other objects. See *Java Distributed Computing*, by Jim Farley (O'Reilly) for more complete coverage of RMI.

Distributed Objects with CORBA

As we've just seen, RMI is a distributed object solution that works well when both client and server are written in Java. It does not work, however, in heterogenous environments where clients and servers may be written in arbitrary languages. For environments like these, the Java 2 platform includes a CORBA-based distributed object solution.

CORBA (Common Object Request Broker Architecture) is a widely used standard defined by the Object Management Group (OMG). This standard is implemented as a core part of the Java 2 platform in the `org.omg.CORBA` package and its subpackages. The implementation includes an Object Request Broker (ORB) that a Java application can use to communicate, as both a client and a server, with other ORBs, and thus with other CORBA objects.

The interfaces to remote CORBA objects are described in a platform- and language-independent way with the Interface Description Language (IDL). The Java Development Kit (JDK) shipped by Sun includes an IDL compiler that translates an IDL description of a remote interface into the Java stub classes necessary to implement the IDL interface in Java or to connect to a remote implementation of the interface from your Java code.

Naming and Directories

The Java Naming and Directory Interface (JNDI) API is a protocol-independent interface to network name services and directory services. For example, it allows arbitrary Java objects to be looked up by name or searched for according to specified attribute values. JNDI is implemented in the `javax.jndi` package as a standard extension to the Java 2 platform.

The JNDI API is not specific to any particular name or directory server protocol. Instead, it is a generic API that is general enough to work with any name or directory server. To support a particular protocol, plug a service provider for that protocol into a JNDI installation. Service providers have been implemented for most common protocols, such as LDAP, DNS, and NIS.

Electronic Mail

The JavaMail API is a protocol-independent interface to electronic mail services. It contains all the features required to send and receive electronic mail, as well as features for filing and searching email. JavaMail is implemented in the `javax.mail` package (and subpackages) as a standard extension to the Java 2 platform.

Like JNDI, the JavaMail API is not tied to any one protocol for sending or receiving email. Instead, the JavaMail API is general enough to work with any email protocol. To support a particular protocol, plug a service provider for that protocol into a JavaMail installation. Sun supplies service providers for the SMTP and IMAP protocols, and, as of this writing, a POP3 provider is under development.

Enterprise JavaBeans

Enterprise JavaBeans do for server-side enterprise programs what JavaBeans do for client-side GUIs. Enterprise JavaBeans (EJB) is a component model for units of business logic and business data. Thin client programming models that take business logic out of the client and put it on a server or in a middle tier have many advantages in enterprise applications. However, the task of writing this middleware has always been complicated by the fact that business logic must be mixed in with code for handling transactions, security, networking, and so on.

The EJB model separates high-level business logic from low-level housekeeping chores. A bean in the EJB model is purely business logic or business data. There are actually two types of beans: *session beans* represent a process or interaction with a client, and *entity beans* represent persistent data stored in a database. EJB beans run within an EJB container, which in turn runs within an EJB server. The container and server provide features such as security, transactional integrity, lifecycle management, name services, distribution services, and so on. The beans running within the container are free to focus purely on business logic.

The EJB specification is a document that specifies the contracts to be maintained and conventions to be followed by EJB servers, containers, and beans. Writing EJB beans is easy: you simply write code to implement your business logic, taking care to follow the rules and conventions imposed by the EJB model. The `javax.ejb` and `javax.ejb.deployment` packages are standard extensions to the Java 2 platform that contain the classes needed to write and deploy EJB beans. The EJB architecture also relies on the JNDI standard extension described earlier, as well as another standard extension known as Java Transaction Services, or JTS.

Of course, writing an EJB bean is not the end of the story. You must also obtain an EJB server and EJB container in which to run the bean. As you might guess from their previous descriptions, these can be very complex pieces of software. An enterprise typically purchases a commercial EJB server and container that implement whatever features are required for its applications. A number of vendors have adapted or are currently adapting their server products to work with Enterprise JavaBeans.

Servlets

A *servlet* is a piece of Java code that runs within a server to provide a service to a client. The name servlet is a takeoff on "applet"—a servlet is a server-side applet. The Java Servlet API provides a generic mechanism for extending the functionality of any kind of server that uses a protocol based on requests and responses.

Right now, servlets are in use primarily by web servers. On the growing number of web servers that support them, servlets are a Java-based replacement for CGI scripts. They can also replace competing technologies, such as ASP or Server-Side JavaScript. The advantage of servlets over these other technologies is that servlets are portable among operating systems and among servers. Servlets are persistent between invocations, which gives them major performance benefits over CGI programs. Servlets also have full access to the rest of the Java platform, so things like database access are automatically supported. For more information on servlets, see *Java Servlet Programming*, by Jason Hunter with William Crawford (O'Reilly).

The Servlet API is a standard extension to the Java 2 platform, implemented in the javax.servlet and javax.servlet.http packages. The javax.servlet package defines classes that represent generic client requests and server responses. The javax.servlet.http package provides specific support for the HTTP protocol, including classes for tracking multiple client requests that are all part of a single client session.

But Wait, There's More!

The core APIs in the Java 2 platform are mature, and I'd say we can expect that core to remain fairly stable in future releases. But obviously there are areas of the Java platform that are still under development. For this reason, the Java 2 platform includes a standard extensions framework for installing and using standard extensions to the platform. Furthermore, Sun has documented and published the process by which proposed extensions become standard extensions.

As we've seen in this chapter, there are already a number of important standard extensions to the Java 2 platform. There are a number of others in various stages of development, and we can expect to see continued activity in this area. I'm going to conclude this overview of the Java 2 platform by mentioning some of the important standard extensions that are under development:

Advanced Imaging API
Provides high-end, state-of-the-art image-processing capabilities, including support for arbitrarily large images using a tile-based storage mechanism.

Java Speech
Offers an API for speech synthesis and voice recognition systems.

Java Telephony
Provides an API for computer-based telephony applications.

Project X
    The code name for an extension that supports the XML markup language.

Java Communications API
    Allows Java to use the serial and parallel ports of the host computer.

Jini
    An innovative and exciting set of packages that enable "plug-and-play" networking among computers, computer peripherals, and consumer electronic devices.

Java Message Service
    Provides an API for enterprise-level asynchronous exchange of messages.

Java Transaction Service/Java Transaction API
    These APIs define a transaction manager and an API for communicating with it. They implement the X/Open XA and OMG OTS standards for transaction management.

Java Electronic Commerce Framework
    A framework that enables electonic commerce, using a "wallet" metaphor on the client side.

Java Management API
    Defines APIs for centralized management of a dynamic and distributed Java computing environment.

CHAPTER 2

How to Use the CD-ROM

The APIs of the Java 2 platform are comparable in breadth and depth to those of a modern, full-featured operating system. The number of packages and classes is large, and the territory they cover is vast. Think of the material on the *Java Power Reference* CD-ROM as an atlas for the Java 2 platform. It is a collection of maps that provide a bird's-eye view of the platform. The atlas lays the APIs out before you, guides you through them, and opens them up for your exploration.

Contents of the Atlas

Just as an atlas contains maps drawn to different scales, the CD-ROM contains quick-reference pages at different levels of abstraction, as shown in Figure 2-1. The three levels of abstraction are:

Platform map
> This is the highest level of abstraction. The platform map summarizes the entire Java 2 platform and its standard extensions by organizing packages into functionally related groups. This map is the table of contents for the atlas— the starting point for your explorations of Java 2.

Package maps
> One level down, we have the package maps. Each package map displays a list of all the Java classes and interfaces contained in a single package. Each map begins with an alphabetical list of the classes and interfaces in the package. That alphabetical listing is followed by a functional listing that groups classes and interfaces by type and by inheritance hierarchy.

Class maps
> This is the lowest level of abstraction. It describes a single class or interface and provides a synopsis of all fields and methods of that class or interface. This is also the most commonly used map, and the map that is most densely packed with information. The bulk of this chapter is an explanation of how to use the information provided in these class maps.

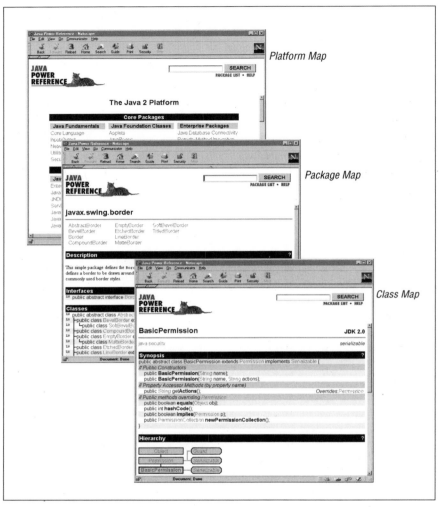

Figure 2-1: The maps of the Java Power Reference

Opening the Atlas

The maps contained in the atlas are HTML pages, designed to be viewed with a web browser. To start using the *Java Power Reference*, simply point your web browser to the *index.htm* file on the CD-ROM. This file contains a link to the *Java Power Reference* itself and also contains links to an online version of this booklet. Click on the *Java Power Reference*, and your browser will open the platform map for the Java 2 platform. You may want to bookmark that page.

For best results, you should use a web browser that supports JavaScript 1.1. We recommend using Netscape Navigator 4 or later or Internet Explorer 4 or later.

The *Java Power Reference* is intended for frequent use while you program. To ensure the quickest access to it, you may want to copy the HTML files from the CD to your hard disk. Beware, however, that the files require over 75 MB of disk space. Also, please note that you are only allowed to copy the files to the hard disk of your own computer, not to computers that belong to your friends or colleagues. Similarly, you are not allowed to redistribute the files over a network.

Navigating the Atlas

The *Java Power Reference* CD-ROM is fully hyperlinked. From the platform map, you can click on the name of any package to see the package map for that package. From a package map, you can click on the name of any class or interface to see the class map for that class. A class map usually contains many links to other related class maps; you can follow those links directly, without going back through the platform map and package map.

The hyperlinks go in the other direction as well. From a class map, you can always follow a link back to the package map for the package that contains the class. And from any class map or package map, you can follow a link back to the top-level platform map. In addition to the hyperlinks, you can always use the **Back** and **Forward** buttons in your browser.

The hyperlinks have another function as well. In order to keep the maps succinct and usable, classes and interfaces are listed without their package names. In other words, a link to the java.lang.String class simply says String, instead of spelling out the full name of the class. However, when you place the mouse over the String hyperlink, the full name of the class appears in the status line of your browser. (If it doesn't, you are probably using a very old browser or you have JavaScript turned off.) Having the package name of a class or interface appear in the status line can be very useful. For example, before following a link to the List class, you may want to check whether it refers to java.awt.List or java.util.List.

In many situations, the easiest way to navigate through this atlas is to use the search capability to jump directly to a particular map. The search capability is the index of the atlas. Type in the name of the package, class, method, or field you are interested in, and you are taken to the appropriate page (as described in the following section).

Searching the Atlas

One of the most powerful features of the *Java Power Reference* is that you can search it for any named package, class, method, or field. Just enter a name into the search field and hit **Return**. If your search string uniquely identifies a package, class, method, or field, you are taken directly to the appropriate package map or class map. If there is more than one match for your search string, you get a list of hyperlinked matches. Click on any of the links to see further details.

Figure 2-2 shows the search field and the results of a search.

Figure 2-2: Searching the Java Power Reference

Here are some guidelines for searching the *Java Power Reference*:

- The search facility uses JavaScript code. That means that it requires a browser that supports JavaScript 1.1 (i.e., Navigator 3 or later or Internet Explorer 4 or later). If you have turned off JavaScript support in your browser, you'll need to turn it back on for searching to work.

- Searches are not case-sensitive. If you want to see the class map for java.lang.String, you can type "string", "String", or "STRING".

- When searching for a class, type only the class name, not the fully qualified name. In other words, don't type the package name as part of the class name. The *Java Power Reference* does not index classes by their package names, so typing a full name like "java.lang.Thread" does not work. Just type "Thread" instead.

- When searching for a package, type the complete name of the package and the package map for that package will be displayed. Thus, if you type "javax.swing", you are taken to the package map for the javax.swing package.

- You can also enter a single component of a package name to see a list of all packages that contain that component (assuming that there is more than one). For example, if you type "swing", you get a list of all packages that contain "swing" in their names. If you are interested in only these packages, this may be a more useful listing to you than the listing provided by the top-level platform map.

- To search for a method or field, type the unqualified name of the method or field. In other words, do not include the class or package name. Because the Java 2 API is so large, there is often more than one method or field with a given name. This means that when searching for a method or field, you are often presented with a list of links to choose from, instead of having a single unique match displayed for you.

- Remember that the *Java Power Reference* does not display individual quick-reference pages for methods and fields. When you search for a method or field, the search results direct you to the appropriate method or field synopsis within the class map of the class that contains the method or field. Also, remember that Java classes may contain more than one method with the same name.

- You can follow your search string with the wildcard character *, which matches anything. For example, if you search for "thread", you see the class map for the java.lang.Thread class. If you search for "thread*", however, you are given a list of links to the Thread, ThreadDeath, ThreadGroup, and ThreadLocal classes. And if you search for "thr*", you get links to those four classes plus the Throwable class.

- If you put an * at the beginning of your search string, you get results that approximate a wildcard search. Normally, the *Java Power Reference* searches for package, class, method, or field names that match your search string exactly. If you begin the search string with an *, it also looks for packages, classes, methods, and fields that contain your search string as a "subword." Many Java class, method, and field names contain multiple words, where each word starts with an capital letter. For example, the ThreadLocal class has a name that contains two words. So, if you search for the string "*local", you find the classes ThreadLocal and InheritableThreadLocal, along with quite a few methods and fields that have the word "local" in their name.

- Remember that placing an * at the beginning of a search string does not result in a fully general wildcard search. For example, the search string "*local" matches a method named isLocal(), but does not match a method named islocal(). Because "islocal" does not have mixed-case capitalization, it does not have "local" as a subword. Placing an * at the beginning of a search string simply makes the search algorithm consider subwords within class, method, and field names. This yields results that are similar to, but not the same as, a true wildcard search.

- You can place an * at both the beginning and the end of a search string. If you search for "*str*", the *Java Power Reference* looks for package, class, method, and field names that start with "str" or that contain a subword that starts with "str". Search targets that begin and end with * can sometimes return too many results to be really useful. "*str*" is such a target. It returns many matches, including classes such as String, StringBuffer, StringReader, Stroke, KeyStroke, and DynStruct.

- The * character is allowed only at the beginning or end of a search string. You may not use it in the middle of a string.

- The *Java Power Reference* search capability works like an index. Like the index of a printed book, you can use it only to search for a single word at a time. Do not try to use it like an Internet search engine that accepts multiple words and phrases.

The Platform Map

The platform map, shown in Figure 2-3, is the highest-level view of the Java platform. It begins with a table of functional groups of packages. Clicking on a group links you to a table of packages in the group. From here, you can click on an individual package name to view the package map for that package. The platform map is organized functionally rather than alphabetically because there are simply too many packages for an alphabetical list to be useful. The functional organization is ideal when you are exploring the Java platform. On the other hand, if you already know exactly which package you are interested in, the quickest way to get there is usually to type its name into the search field and hit **Return**.

Package Maps

A package map summarizes the contents of one package of the Java platform. An example is shown in Figure 2-4. Each package map begins with an alphabetical listing of the classes and interfaces in the package. If you already know the name of the class you are looking for, this alphabetical listing makes it easy to find. (Remember, too, that you can search for a class by name using the search field.)

The alphabetical class listing is followed by a short package description. This description briefly explains the purpose of the package and lists the most important classes and interfaces in it. It gives you a starting place for your explorations of the package.

The package description is followed by a functional listing of the package contents. In this section, classes and interfaces are grouped by category, rather than by name. For example, all exception classes in a package are grouped together, as are all event classes, component classes, and collection classes. In addition to this grouping by category, classes are arranged into a class hierarchy, with subclasses following their superclass and indented with respect to that superclass.

The purpose of this functional grouping of classes and interfaces is to make it easier to understand the organization and contents of the package. It also serves as a better starting point for your explorations of the package. If you don't already know the name of the class or interface you are looking for, you will find the functional organization more useful than the alphabetical listing.

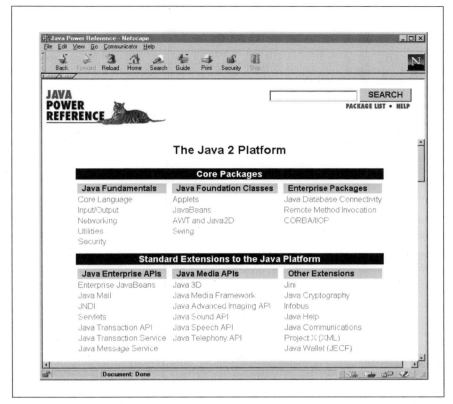

Figure 2-3: The platform map

Class Maps

A class map summarizes the contents of one class or interface of the Java platform. Class maps typically contain more information than the platform map or package maps. Each class map contains a number of sections, and each section contains a specific type of information. Some of this information is quite dense and requires detailed explanation. The sections that follow explain the layout of a class map step by step.

Class Title

Each class map begins with a title section that contains the name of the class and other high-level class details, as Figure 2-5 illustrates. As you can see, the name of the class appears in the top left of this section. The name of the package that contains the class appears in a smaller font beneath the class name. The package name is a hyperlink, providing an easy way to move from a class map to the containing package map.

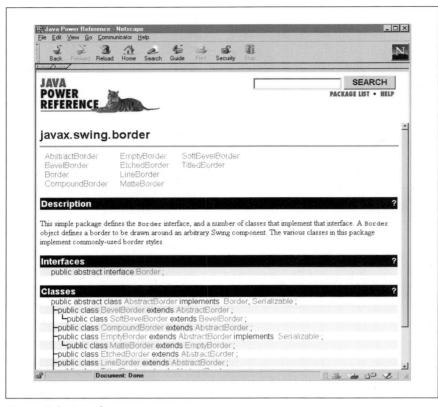

Figure 2-4: A package map

Figure 2-5: The class title section of a class map

The top right of the title section contains version information for the class. This specifies the first release of the Java Development Kit that contained the class. Or, for standard extensions that are released independently of the JDK, it specifies the first version of the extension that contained the class. In addition, if the class or interface has been deprecated, that fact is also noted in the top right of the title section.

Finally, the area beneath the version number contains class flags that specify high-level information about a class. Flags such as "collection," "Swing component," and "event listener" specify a general category for the class. Flags such as "serializable," "cloneable," "runnable," and "accessible" specify common interfaces implemented by the class. For exception classes, the flags "checked" and "unchecked" specify whether the exception must be declared in the throws clause of a method that may throw it.

Class Synopsis

The title section is followed by the synopsis section, which is really the heart of a class map. This section contains the Java API that is defined by the class or interface. Using standard Java syntax, this section displays the class declaration followed by the signatures of all of the fields, methods, and inner classes defined by the class. Figure 2-6 shows the synopsis section for a relatively simple class; in larger classes, the synopsis section can be substantially longer.

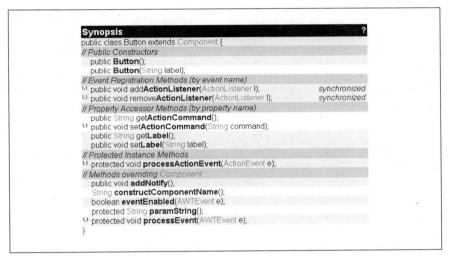

Figure 2-6: The synopsis section of a class map

The first line of the synopsis section is the class declaration itself. This line includes class modifiers such as public and abstract, defines the superclass of the class, and lists the interfaces that it implements. This is high-level information about the class as a whole. The remainder of the synopsis is API information about the members (methods, fields, and inner classes) of the class.

Functional grouping of members

The first thing to note about the member API information is that the members are grouped functionally rather than alphabetically. Constructors, methods, fields, and inner classes are all listed separately. Instance methods are kept separate from static (class) methods. Constants are separated from non-constant fields. Public members are listed separately from protected members. These categorizations of class members should be familiar to readers of *Java in a Nutshell.* Readers have found that grouping members by category breaks a class down into smaller, more comprehensible segments, making the class easier to understand. This grouping also makes it easier for you to find a desired member.

The *Java Power Reference* takes this functional grouping of members a step further. In addition to grouping members by their general type, it also groups them by use or purpose. For example, the property accessor methods used by Swing components and many other classes are functionally related because they all access property values. These methods follow naming conventions that make this relationship even more apparent. The same is true for the event registration methods of Swing and AWT GUI components. The JavaBeans and Swing programming models encourage programmers to think about components and other classes in terms of the properties they define and the events they trigger. Thus, these property accessor methods and event listener registration methods are grouped together into special sections, instead of being mixed in with the other public instance methods defined by the class.

The *Java Power Reference* also groups methods based on hierarchy considerations. When a class implements an interface, it is reasonable to assume that the methods of that interface are functionally related to each other. Thus, these methods are grouped together. Similarly, when a class overrides methods of one of its superclasses, it often overrides a related set of methods. So overriding methods are grouped together, based on the superclass that they override. Even when the overriding methods are not closely related in functional terms, their grouping helps you understand how a class relates to and interacts with its superclass.

There are quite a few functional groupings used for class members in the *Java Power Reference*. Some have a clear purpose and require no explanation. Others are more complex and do require explanation. For completeness, all of the functional categories are listed here, in the order in which they appear in the class synopsis:

Constructors
> Displays the constructors for the class. Public constructors and protected constructors are displayed separately in subgroupings. If a class defines no constructor at all, the Java compiler adds a default no-argument constructor that is displayed here. If a class defines only private constructors, it cannot be instantiated, so a special, empty grouping entitled "No Constructor" indicates this fact. Constructors are listed first because the first thing you do with most classes is instantiate them by calling a constructor.

Constants
> Displays all of the constants (i.e., fields that are declared static and final) defined by the class. Public and protected constants are displayed in separate subgroups. Constants are listed here, near the top of the class synopsis, because constant values are often used throughout the class as legal values for method parameters and return values.

Inner Classes
> Groups all of the inner classes and interfaces defined by the class or interface. For each inner class, there is a single-line synopsis. Each inner class also has its own class map that includes a full class synopsis for the inner class. Like constants, inner classes are listed near the top of the class synopsis because they are often used by a number of other members of the class.

Static Methods

Lists the static methods (class methods) of the class, broken down into subgroups for public static methods and protected static methods.

Event Listener Registration Methods

Lists the public instance methods that register and deregister event listener objects with the class. The names of these methods begin with the words "add" and "remove" and end in "Listener". These methods are always passed a java.util.EventListener object. The methods are typically defined in pairs, so the pairs are listed together. The methods are listed alphabetically by event name, rather than by method name.

Property Accessor Methods

Lists the public instance methods that set or query the value of a property or attribute of the class. The names of these methods begin with the words "set," "get," and "is," and their signatures follow the patterns set out in the JavaBeans specification. Although the naming conventions and method signature patterns are defined for JavaBeans, classes and interfaces throughout the Java platform define property accessor methods that follow these conventions and patterns. Looking at a class in terms of the properties it defines can be a powerful tool for understanding the class, so property methods are grouped together in this section.

Property accessor methods are listed alphabetically by property name, not by method name. This means that the "set," "get," and "is" methods for a property all appear together. The *Java Power Reference* defines a property accessor method in a somewhat more general way than the JavaBeans specification does. A method is considered to be a property accessor if it follows the JavaBeans conventions itself or if it has the same name as a method that follows those conventions. Consider the setSize() method of the Component class. There are two versions of this method, and, since they have the same name, they obviously share a purpose and deserve to be grouped together. However, only one version of the method strictly follows the JavaBeans signature patterns. The relaxed definition of what constitutes a property accessor method allows these two methods to be listed together, as they should be.

Instance Methods

Contains all of the instance methods that are not event registration methods or property accessor methods and that do not implement an interface or override a method of a superclass. The methods are broken into public and protected subgroups.

Implementing Methods

Groups the methods that implement the same interface. There is one subgroup for each interface implemented by the class. Methods that are defined by the same interface are almost always related to each other, so this is a useful functional grouping of methods.

Note that if an interface method is also an event registration method or a property accessor method, it is listed both in this group and in the event or property group. This situation does not arise often, but when it does, all of the functional groupings are important and useful enough to warrant the duplicate listing. When an interface method is listed in the event or property group, it displays an "Implements:" flag that specifies the name of the interface of which it is part.

Overriding Methods

Groups the methods that override methods of a superclass broken down into subgroups by superclass. This is typically a useful grouping, because it helps to make it clear how a class modifies the default behavior of its superclasses. In practice, it is also often true that methods that override the same superclass are functionally related to each other.

Sometimes a method that overrides a superclass is also a property accessor method or (more rarely) an event registration method. When this happens, the method is grouped with the property or event methods and displays a flag that indicates which superclass it overrides. The method is not listed with other overriding methods, however. Note that this is different from interface methods, which, because they are more strongly functionally related, may have duplicate listings in both groups.

Static Fields

Lists any static class fields that are not constants, breaking them into public and protected subgroups. In practice, static fields are fairly rare. They are listed near the bottom of the class synopsis because they are usually less important than the constructors, constants, inner classes, and methods that precede them.

Instance Fields

Contains any instance fields defined by the class, breaking them into public and protected subgroups. Many classes define no such accessible fields. For those that do, many object-oriented programmers prefer not to use those fields directly, but instead to use accessor methods when such methods are available.

Deprecated Members

Deprecated methods and deprecated fields are grouped at the very bottom of the class synopsis. Use of these methods and fields is strongly discouraged.

Member flags

Within a class synopsis, member synopses are grouped as explained previously. Each member synopsis is a single line that defines the API for that member. These synopses use Java syntax, so their meaning is immediately clear to any Java programmer. There is some auxiliary information associated with each member synopsis, however, that requires explanation.

Recall that a class map begins with a title section that includes the release in which the class was first defined. When a member is introduced into a class after the initial release of the class, the version in which the member was introduced appears, in small print, to the left of the member synopsis. Furthermore, if a member has been deprecated, that fact is indicated with a hash mark (#) to the left of the member synopsis.

The area to the right of the member synopsis is used to display a variety of member flags that provide additional information about the member. Some of these flags provide additional specification details that do not appear in the member API itself. Other flags contain implementation-specific information. This information can be quite useful in understanding the class and in debugging, but it may differ between implementations. The implementation-specific flags displayed in the *Java Power Reference* are based on Sun's implementation of Java for Microsoft Windows.

The following flags may be displayed to the right of a member synopsis:

native
> An implementation-specific flag that indicates that a method is implemented in native code. Although native is a Java keyword and can appear in method signature, it is part of the method implementation, not part of its specification. Therefore, this information is included with the member flags, rather than as part of the member synopsis. This flag is useful as a hint about the expected performance of a method.

synchronized
> An implementation-specific flag that indicates that a method implementation is declared synchronized, meaning that it obtains a lock on the object or class before executing. Like the native keyword, the synchronized keyword is part of the method implementation, not part of the specification, so it appears as a flag, not in the method synopsis itself. This flag is a useful hint that the method is probably implemented in a thread-safe manner.

> Whether or not a method is thread-safe is part of the method specification, and this information *should* appear (although it often does not) in the method documentation. There are a number of different ways to make a method thread-safe, however, and declaring the method with the synchronized keyword is only one possible implementation. In other words, a method that does not bear the synchronized keyword can still be thread-safe.

Overrides:
> Indicates that a method overrides a method in one of its superclasses. The flag is followed by the name of the superclass that the method overrides. This is a specification detail, not an implementation detail. This flag is used only when the overriding method is grouped with event registration or property accessor methods. As explained in the discussion of functional grouping of methods, overriding methods are usually grouped in a special section based on the superclass they override. In these sections, the "Overrides:" flag is not necessary.

Implements:
> Indicates that a method implements a method in an interface. The flag is followed by the name of the interface that is implemented. This is a specification detail, not an implementation detail. Because methods that implement interface methods are grouped into special sections, this flag is used only when the method is duplicated in the event registration or property accessor section.

empty

Indicates that the implementation of the method has an empty body. This can be a hint to the programmer that the method may need to be overridden in a subclass. The `Applet.init()` method is a good example of this type of method.

constant

An implementation flag that indicates that a method has a trivial implementation. Only methods with a `void` return type can be truly empty. Any method declared to return a value must have at least a `return` statement. The "constant" flag indicates that the method implementation is empty except for a `return` statement that returns a constant value. Such a method might have a body like `return null;` or `return false;`. Like the "empty" flag, this flag indicates that a method may need to be overridden.

default:

Used with property accessor methods that read the value of a property. The flag is followed by the default value of the property. Strictly speaking, default property values are a specification detail. In practice, however, these defaults are not always documented, and care should be taken, because the default values may change between implementations.

Not all properties have a "default:" flag. A default value is determined by dynamically loading the class in question, instantiating it using a no-argument constructor, and then calling the property "get" method to find out what it returns. This technique can be used only on classes that can be dynamically loaded and instantiated and that have no-argument constructors, so default values are shown for those classes only. Furthermore, note that when a class is instantiated using a different constructor, the default values for its properties may be different.

bound

Indicates that a property is a bound property. In other words, the class generates a `java.beans.PropertyChangeEvent` when the property changes. This is a specification detail, but it is sometimes not documented. Information about bound properties is obtained from the `BeanInfo` object for the class.

.constrained

Indicates that a property is constrained. In other words, the property setter method may throw a `java.beans.PropertyVetoException`. This is a specification detail, not an implementation detail.

expert

Indicates that the `BeanInfo` object for this class specifies that this property or event is intended for use by experts only. This hint is intended for visual programming tools, but users of the *Java Power Reference* may find the hint useful as well.

hidden

Indicates that the `BeanInfo` object for this class specifies that this property or event is for internal use only. This is a hint that visual programming tools should hide the property or event from the programmer. The *Java Power Ref-*

erence does not hide these properties and events, of course, but this flag does indicate that you should probably avoid using the property or event.

preferred

> Indicates that the BeanInfo object for this class specifies that the property or event is in some way the default or preferred property or event. This is a hint to visual programming tools to display the property or event in a prominent way, and it is also a useful hint to users of the *Java Power Reference.*

=

> For constant fields, this flag is followed by the constant value of the field. Only constants of primitive types and constants with the value null are displayed. Some constant values are specification details, while others are implementation details. The reason that symbolic constants are defined, however, is so you can write code that does not rely directly upon the constant value. Use this flag to help you understand the class, but do not rely upon the constant values in your own programs.

Class Hierarchy

Now that we've examined the functional grouping of members and member flags within the class synopsis, let's pull back and look at the whole picture of a class map again. Each class map begins with a title section, followed by the synopsis section. While the synopsis contains the bulk of the information about the class, it does not contain all of the information. The synopsis section is followed by a hierarchy diagram, like the one pictured in Figure 2-7.

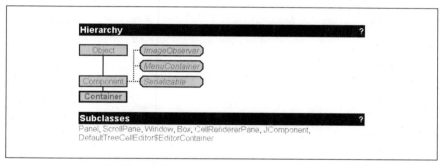

Figure 2-7: The hierarchy and subclasses sections of a class map

As you can see, the hierarchy diagram for a class displays all of the superclasses of the class, all of the interfaces it implements, as well as all of the interfaces implemented by each of its superclasses. The rectangular boxes along the left edge of the diagram form the class tree. This tree begins with the root class java.lang.Object and moves down through the class hierarchy to the class being documented. To the right of each class, connected by dotted lines, are the interfaces it implements. Interfaces are displayed in octagons, rather than rectangles. Note that interfaces may themselves have interfaces that appear to their right. Interfaces do not have superclasses, so the hierarchy diagram for an interface often consists of only a single octagon.

Subclasses

The hierarchy diagram just described displays the classes and interfaces above a given class in the inheritance hierarchy. The section that follows the diagram lists the classes that appear below it in the hierarchy. If a class has subclasses, or an interface has subinterfaces, the hierarchy diagram is followed by a "Subclasses" section that lists those subclasses or subinterfaces. Figure 2-7 illustrates this "Subclasses" section.

Implementations

Most interfaces do not have subinterfaces, and therefore do not have a "Subclasses" section. Many interfaces, however, do have implementations. All implementations of a given interface are listed in the "Implementations" section.

Properties Table

The "Hierarchy," "Subclasses," and "Implementations" sections are followed by a section entitled "JavaBeans Properties." This section contains a summary table of the properties defined by the class or interface. For each property, the table lists the property name, its type, its accessor methods, its default value, and any relevant flags. Figure 2-8 shows what such a table looks like.

JavaBeans Properties				
Name	**Type**	**Access**	**Default**	**Flags**
alignmentX	float	get	0.5	read-only
alignmentY	float	get	0.5	read-only
componentCount	int	get	0	read-only
components	Component[]	get		read-only
font	Font	set		write-only
insets	Insets	get		read-only
layout	LayoutManager	get / set	null	
maximumSize	Dimension	get		read-only
minimumSize	Dimension	get		read-only
preferredSize	Dimension	get		read-only

Figure 2-8: The property table section of a class map

Inherited Members

The synopsis section of a class map lists only the members implemented directly by a class. Of course, when you are using the class, you can also use members that are inherited by the class from its superclasses. The next three sections in a class map display these inherited methods, under the titles "Inherited Properties," "Inherited Events," and "Inherited Methods." Figure 2-9 shows what one of these sections looks like.

Each section displays the appropriate inherited members broken down by the superclass from which they are inherited. The sections list inherited properties, events, and methods; they do not provide synopses for them. If you need more information about one, you need to visit the class map of the superclass from which it is inherited.

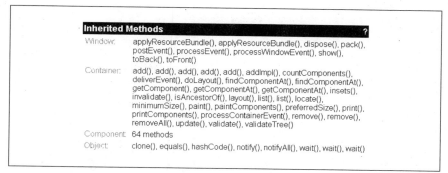

Figure 2-9: The inherited methods section of a class map

Some classes such as `java.awt.Component` define a huge number of methods, and a complete listing of inherited methods would be too long to be useful. In this case, the method list is omitted.

Cross References

The final sections of a class map are the cross references. These sections list the other classes, methods, and fields that use the class in some way. Some classes, such as `java.lang.String`, are so widely used that the cross reference lists become too long to be useful. In cases like these, the cross reference lists are omitted. Figure 2-10 shows what some of these sections look like.

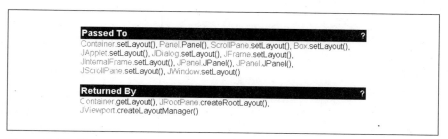

Figure 2-10: Two cross reference sections of a class map

The *Java Power Reference* provides the following cross reference sections:

Passed To
    Displays a list of methods that take a parameter of this type.

Returned By
    Displays a list of methods that return a value of this type.

Thrown By
    For error and exception classes, displays a list of methods that throw the error or exception.

Type Of

Displays a list of fields of this type.

Uses

Displays a list of classes and interfaces that this class uses. This section is different from the others, in that it contains implementation-level information obtained by scanning the bytecode of the class. As a result, this list may contain classes that do not appear anywhere in the public API (the specification) of the class.

Used By

Displays the reverse of the "Uses" section. It lists classes that use this class in their implementation. The classes that appear in this list may not use this class in their public API (specification).

Index

Symbols

* wildcard, 33

A

accessibility, 14
Action interface, 16
actions, 16
Advanced Imaging API, 27
Applet class, 18
applets, 10, 18
    server-side (servlets), 27
atlas on CD-ROM, 29–34
    class maps, 29, 35–46
    navigating, 31
    package maps, 29, 34
    platform map, 29, 34
    searching, 31–34
audio, 23
    JMF (Java Media Framework), 23
    three-dimensional, 23

B

beans, 18–19
    EJB (Enterprise JavaBeans), 26
borders on Swing components, 16
bound flag, 42
Box component (Swing), 10
business logic management, 26
button components (Swing), 10

C

case insensitivity of atlas searches, 32
checkbox components (Swing), 10
class hierarchy, 43
class maps (CD-ROM atlas), 29, 35–46
classes, 6
ClassLoader class, 9
code permissions, 9
collections classes, 8
color, 20
color chooser components (Swing), 11
ColorSpace object, 20
combination box components
    (Swing), 11
Common Object Request Broker
    Architecture (CORBA), 25
compressing data streams, 7
constant flag, 42
constants, 38
constrained flag, 42
constructors, 38
CORBA, 25
cross references, 45
cryptography, 9

D

data structures, 8
database access, 24
DatagramPacket class, 8
DatagramSocket class, 8

decompressing data streams, 7
decryption, 9
default: flag, 42
deprecated members, 40
desktop panes (Swing), 11
dialog boxes (Swing), 11
digital signatures, 9
directory services, 25
distributed objects
    CORBA for, 25
    RMI for, 24
drag-and-drop, 17, 19
Driver class, 24
dynamic programming, 4

E

editor panes (Swing), 11
efficiency of programming, 5
EJB (Enterprise JavaBeans), 26
electronic mail services, 26
empty flag, 42
encryption, 9
Enterprise APIs, 23–27
    EJB (Enterprise JavaBeans), 26
entity beans (EJB), 26
event listener registration methods, 39
expert flag, 42
extensibility, 4

F

fields, searching atlas for, 33
file choosers (Swing), 11
File classes, 7
fonts, 20
frame components (Swing), 11

G

graphical user interface, 9–19
    drag-and-drop, 17, 19
    pluggable look-and-feel, 14
graphics, 19–23
    Java 2D graphics model, 20
    Java 3D API, 22
GUI (graphical user interface), 9–19
    drag-and-drop, 17, 19
    pluggable look-and-feel, 14
GZIP compression format, 7

H

help package, 18
hidden flag, 42
hierarchy of classes, 43
hyperlink in atlas, 31

I

IDL (Interface Description Language),
    25
image processing, 21
implementations of interfaces, 44
implementing methods, 39
Implements: flag, 41
infobus architecture, 19
inherited members, 44
inner classes, 38
input methods, 17
input/output, 6
instance fields, 40
instance methods, 39
Interface Description Language (IDL),
    25
interface implementations, 44
internal frames (Swing), 11
internationalization, 4, 8
    input method support, 17

J

JAF (Java Activation Framework), 19
JApplet class, 18
JApplet component (Swing), 10
JAR archive format, 7
Java
    benefits of, 3–5
    graphics features, 19–23
    GUI (graphical user interface), 9–19
    language vs. platform, 1
    naming the Java 2 platform, 5
    O'Reilly on, ix
    version history, vii
Java 2 features, 6–9
Java 2D graphics model, 20
Java 3D API, 22
Java Activation Framework (JAF), 19
Java Communications API, 28
Java Cryptography Extension (JCE), 9

Java Database Connectivity (JDBC), 24
Java Development Kit (JDK), 25
Java Enterprise APIs, 23–27
    EJB (Enterprise JavaBeans), 26
Java Media Framework (JMF), 23
Java Naming and Directory Interface
    (JNDI), 25
Java RMI (Remote Method Invocation),
    24
Java Servlet API, 27
Java Speech, 27
Java Telephony, 27
java.awt package, 20
    java.awt.Color, 20
    java.awt.font, 20
    java.awt.image, 21
    java.awt.print, 22
java.awt.im package, 17
JavaBeans system, 18–19
    EJB (Enterprise JavaBeans), 26
JavaHelp extension, 18
java.io package, 6
java.lang package, 6
java.lang.reflect package, 6
JavaMail API, 26
java.math package, 8
java.net package, 7
    I/O streams and, 7
java.rmi package, 24
java.security package, 9
java.sql package, 24
java.swing.undo package, 16
java.text package, 8, 17
java.util package, 8
java.util.jar package, 7
java.util.zip package, 7
javax.accessibiliy package, 14
javax.activation package, 19
javax.ejb package, 26
javax.infobus package, 19
javax.javahelp package, 18
javax.jndi package, 25
javax.mail package, 26
javax.media.j3d package, 22
javax.servlet package, 27
javax.servlet.http package, 27
javax.sql package, 24
javax.swing package, 10
javax.swing.border package, 16
javax.vecmath package, 23

JButton component (Swing), 10
JCE (Java Cryptography Extension), 9
JCheckBox component (Swing), 10
JCheckBoxMenuItem component
    (Swing), 11
JColorChooser component (Swing), 11
JComboBox component (Swing), 11
JComponent component (Swing), 11
JDBC (Java Database Connectivity), 24
JDesktopPane component (Swing), 11
JDialog component (Swing), 11
JDK (Java Development Kit), 25
JEditorPane component (Swing), 11
JFileChooser component (Swing), 11
JFrame component (Swing), 11
JInternalFrame component (Swing), 11
JLabel component (Swing), 11
JLayeredPane component (Swing), 11
JList component (Swing), 11
JMenu component (Swing), 11
JMenuBar component (Swing), 12
JMenuItem component (Swing), 12
JMF (Java Media Framework), 23
JNDI (Java Naming and Directory
    Interface), 25
JOptionPane component (Swing), 12
JPanel component (Swing), 12
JPasswordField component (Swing),
    12
JPopupMenu component (Swing), 12
JProgressBar component (Swing), 12
JRadioButton component (Swing), 12
JRadioButtonMenuItem component
    (Swing), 12
JRootPane component (Swing), 12
JScrollBar component (Swing), 12
JScrollPane component (Swing), 12
JSeparator component (Swing), 12
JSlider component (Swing), 12
JSplitPane component (Swing), 12
JTabbedPane component (Swing), 12
JTable component (Swing), 13
JTextArea component (Swing), 13
JTextComponent component (Swing),
    13
JTextField component (Swing), 13
JTextPane component (Swing), 13
JToggleButton component (Swing), 13
JToolBar component (Swing), 13
JToolTip component (Swing), 13

JTree component (Swing), 13
JViewport component (Swing), 13
JWindow component (Swing), 13

K

key certificates, 9
keyboard traversal, 17

L

label components (Swing), 11
layered panes (Swing), 11
list components (Swing), 11
localization, 4, 8
    input method support, 17
look-and-feel, 14

M

mail services, 26
mathematics, 8
member flags, 40
members, inherited, 44
menu components (Swing), 11
message digests, 9
methods, 39
    searching atlas for, 33
model/view architecture, 14
mouse pointers, 21
mouseless GUI operation, 17

N

name and directory services, 25
native members, 41
navigating atlas, 31
networking, 7
    I/O streams and, 7
    Java as network-centric, 4
    name and directory services, 25
    object-oriented programming for,
        24

O

Object Request Broker (ORB), 25
ObjectInputStream class, 7
object-oriented network programming,
    24
ObjectOutputStream class, 7
opening atlas, 30

option panes (Swing), 12
ORB (Object Request Broker), 25
org.omg.CORBA package, 25
Overrides: flag, 41
overriding methods, 40

P

package maps (CD-ROM atlas), 29, 34
packages, searching atlas for, 32
panel components (Swing), 12
Passed To section, 45
password fields (Swing), 12
Permission class, 9
platform, defined, 2
platform map (CD-ROM atlas), 29, 34
pluggable look-and-feel, 14
Policy class, 9
popup menus (Swing), 12
portability, 3
preferred flag, 43
printing, 22
private keys, 9
progress bars (Swing), 12
Project X, 28
properties, 44
property accessor methods, 39
public key cryptography, 9

R

radio buttons (Swing), 12
RandomAccessFile class, 7
reader classes, 6
redo/undo framework, 16
Remote Method Invocation (RMI), 24
Returned By section, 45
RGB color space, 20
RMI (Remote Method Invocation), 24
root panes (Swing), 12
runtime environment, defined, 2

S

scroll panes (Swing), 12
scrollbar components (Swing), 12
searching atlas, 31–34
security, 3, 9
    networking, 8
SecurityManager class, 9
separator components (Swing), 12

serialization, 7
ServerSocket class, 8
servlets, 27
sessions beans (EJB), 26
Shape objects, 20
slider components (Swing), 12
Socket class, 8
sound, 23
    JMF (Java Media Framework), 23
    three-dimensional, 23
split panes (Swing), 12
state, component (Swing), 14
static fields, 40
static methods, 39
streams, input/output, 6
subclasses, 44
Swing components
    model/view architecture, 14
    pluggable look-and-feel, 14
Swing library, 10–17
    components of, 10–13
    features, 16
synchronized methods, 41

T

tabbed panes (Swing), 12
table components (Swing), 13
text components (Swing), 13
three-dimensional graphics, 22
Thrown By section, 45
Timer class, 16
timers, 16
time-to-market, 5

toggle buttons (Swing), 13
toolbar components (Swing), 13
tooltips, 13, 16
tree components (Swing), 13
two-dimensional graphics, 20
Type Of section, 46

U

undo framework, 16
Used By section, 46
user interface, 9–19
    drag-and-drop, 17, 19
    pluggable look-and-feel, 14
Uses section, 46
utility classes, 8

V

version history of Java, vii
version number confusion with Java 2,
    5
video, JMF for, 23
viewport components (Swing), 13

W

wildcards in atlas searches, 33
window components (Swing), 13
"Write once, run anywhere", 3
writer classes, 6

Z

ZIP compression format, 7

About the Author

David Flanagan is a computer programmer who spends most of his time writing about Java. His previous books for O'Reilly & Associates include *Java in a Nutshell*, *Java Examples in a Nutshell*, and *JavaScript: The Definitive Guide*. David has a degree in computer science and engineering from the Massachusetts Institute of Technology. He lives with his partner, Christie, in the Pacific Northwest, between the cities of Seattle and Vancouver.

Colophon

Our look is the result of reader comments, our own experimentation, and feedback from distribution channels. Distinctive covers complement our distinctive approach to technical topics, breathing personality and life into potentially dry subjects.

Nancy Kotary was the production editor and copyeditor for *Introduction to the Java 2 Platform*; Sheryl Avruch was the production manager; Madeleine Newell and Sarah Jane Shangraw provided quality control. Robert Romano created the illustrations using Adobe Photoshop 4 and Macromedia FreeHand 7. Lenny Muellner provided technical support. Seth Maislin wrote the index.

Edie Freedman and Kathleen Wilson designed the packaging graphics for the Java Power Reference and the book cover for *Introducing the Java 2 Platform*. The tiger image is Copyright © Photodisc 1999 and is used with permission. QuarkXPress 3.32 and Photoshop 5.02 were used to create the artwork, with ITC Garamond and Bitstream Futura fonts. Title pages were created by Alicia Cech.

The inside layout was designed by Nancy Priest and implemented in SGML by Lenny Muellner. The text and heading fonts are ITC Garamond Light and Garamond Book.

Whenever possible, our books use RepKover™, a durable and flexible lay-flat binding. If the page count exceeds RepKover's limit, perfect binding is used.